'*The Book of Non-Binary Joy* is full of wit, kind advice, encouragement, fun and wisdom! Let Ben take you by the hand for this fabulous ride into the expansiveness of our genders and communities, you will not regret it.'

– Alex Iantaffi, author of *Gender Trauma, How to Understand Your Gender* and *Life Isn't Binary*

'This book speaks directly to the non-binary reader, because let's face it, there aren't many that do, but rest assured it is for everyone. To read, to learn, to understand better another person's perspective is incredibly powerful. This book debunks common misconceptions and gives insightful and useful information that we all need. They discuss trauma and the wider context of living in a world that often doesn't support or accept you with a beautifully delicate, light hand – giving the reader a real sense of pride and joy that is often neglected when talking about these issues.'

– Natalie Lee (Style Me Sunday)

'This book is a joy to read! *The Book of Non-Binary Joy* is in perfect balance: direct, kind and deeply respectful explorations of what it means to be human, mixed with encouraging and purely prideful happiness. Beautifully illustrated and brilliantly witty, this is the book to help everyone expand their gender-delight.'

– Jeffrey Marsh, bestselling author of *How to Be You*

'*The Book of Non-Binary Joy* is just that. JOY. Every page is packed full of love, acceptance, encouragement and more. Ben's wit, charm and warmth leap off the page like a big friendly hug. I know this book will help LGBTQIA+ people on their gender journey and discovery. Thank you Ben, from one of them.'

T0000861

'I'm so happy this book exists. As a trans man, it's a genuinely useful resource and as a trans person, it's a breath of fresh air for the focus to be on our ample, multifaceted joy instead of simply the pain we experience at the hands of cis society.'

— Freddy McConnell, writer and journalist

'Honest, incisive and responsive writing. A commanding and nuanced conversation of representation, allyship and identity...a book I wished I'd had in my twenties.'

— Jules Von Hep, entrepreneur and philanthropist

THE BOOK OF NON-BINARY JOY

of related interest

The Trans Self-Care Workbook
A Coloring Book and Journal for Trans and Non-Binary People
Theo Lorenz
ISBN 978 1 78775 343 3
eISBN 978 1 78775 344 0

Non-Binary Lives
An Anthology of Intersecting Identities
Edited by Jos Twist, Ben Vincent, Meg-John Barker and Kat Gupta
ISBN 978 1 78775 339 6
eISBN 978 1 78775 340 2

In Their Shoes
Navigating Non-Binary Life
Jamie Windust
ISBN 978 1 78775 242 9
eISBN 978 1 78775 243 6

Trans Power
Own Your Gender
Juno Roche
ISBN 978 1 78775 019 7
eISBN 978 1 78775 020 3

The Book *of* Non-Binary *Joy*

Embracing the Power of You

Ben Pechey

Illustrated by Sam Prentice

Jessica Kingsley Publishers
London and Philadelphia

First published in Great Britain in 2022 by Jessica Kingsley Publishers
An imprint of Hodder & Stoughton Ltd
An Hachette Company

4

Copyright © Ben Pechey 2022
Illustrations Copyright © Sam Prentice 2022

A CIP catalogue record for this title is available from the
British Library and the Library of Congress

ISBN 978 1 78775 910 7
eISBN 978 1 78775 911 4

Printed and bound in Great Britain by Clays Ltd

Jessica Kingsley Publishers' policy is to use papers that are natural,
renewable and recyclable products and made from wood grown
in sustainable forests. The logging and manufacturing processes
are expected to conform to the environmental regulations
of the country of origin.

Jessica Kingsley Publishers
Carmelite House
50 Victoria Embankment
London EC4Y 0DZ

www.jkp.com

♡

For you, for me, for all of us.
Always have Hope...

Contents

Introduction

Oh hello darling, and welcome to this, my very first book. It is very important to me that you see the pages of this tome as a safe space. Here you will find no judgement, and no expectations or requirements placed on you, the reader; instead I urge you to see these pages as a guide to unlocking more joy in your own existence.

Many humans find it hard to put themselves first, and sadly as non-binary people we have been conditioned to expect less for ourselves. Clichés are unfairly treated in my opinion, and are overlooked for being obvious. Well, sometimes obvious is good, and helpful, so it is a cliché, but in order to love life, we have to learn first how to love ourselves. At this juncture I have to be honest with you – the pages you are about to devour will have no purpose if you are not willing to love yourself.

This is the one and only change I need you to make – this book is here to help you be yourself. This is not going to require more effort from you, and this is the way it should be. In the past as a community we have had to work our fingers to the bone to carve out space for who we are, and now we have finally covered some ground in terms of rights and quality of life, we need to just start living.

The book in your hands is here to provide knowledge and experiences to help you be you in the best way you want. I haven't sugar-coated my words and, to be frank, some of the conversations I have had on these pages may seem anything but positive, but I promise you, they are necessary.

My biggest regret is that I didn't give myself the space to live my truth at a younger age; instead I waited until I was 21 or 22, and that was partly through my own hang-ups, but also because the conversation and visibility I needed were not there. Remember, you cannot be what you don't know! It took a lot of changes and chance meetings with wonderful queer humans for me to finally honour who I am.

My words may not answer all your questions, or tick all the boxes on the list you have in your head, but they will do a lot of the work for you. There is more than enough to help you if you are right at the start of your journey of self-exploration, and plenty of deeper topics to help you if you have been on the wild ride of gender introspection for longer.

The reality of this situation is that we have known exactly who we are for as long as we can remember. It may have been a looser sense of difference from the mainstream than it is now, but I can guarantee it was there. We may not have had the language to describe that feeling, or had the visibility to be able to voice who we are at an academic level, but we have always been exactly who we are.

My words and my thoughts are here to remind you that in some ways you have always known who you are, and this book is here to help you see how to be you in all your glory, and hopefully with my guidance you can start that journey today, right now.

How to Read This Book

I am well aware that you know how to read, but traditional books give you a framework in which you start on page one, and carry on reading to the end. This book is not the same. You get to choose how you read it.

You can read this book cover to cover, and enjoy me chronologically; this would be a fabulous first introduction to the topic and to who I am. Once you've finished the book, you can go back and reread sections you would like to get to know better. This book is yours and not mine! You could even highlight passages that really resonate with you, unless it's a library book or you borrowed it from a friend, in which case please don't do that – maybe buy your own copy first – it would be a great way to say thank you to me, and my divine editor, Andrew!

It will also work if you pick and choose the sections that call out to you right now. There is no specific order. In reality, you could read one part of a chapter and get all that you might need. You could just go through the contents page and pick where you want to start. Page 72 is really fabulous in my opinion, but you can choose your own starting point, darling. There is no Goosebumps guide throughout the book, partly because that would be copyright infringement, but mainly because this just isn't a scary book.

This book is first and foremost for you, so how you read it is completely up to you. Taking this time just for you is a very important step, so, however you read it, please give yourself the space to digest my words. All I ask is that you go into the reading process with an open mind and an open heart.

I am not an expert with two degrees, a PhD and an honorary doctorate from Oxford; I just have a healthy amount of experience and a great way with words. I want you to get the most that you can out of this book, so you can get the most out of being your true self!

Along the way you will hear from 14 other voices who will offer you their experiences. These wonderful individuals are here to make this book more useful and hopefully even more relatable. All their details will be included at the end of this book so that you can follow them and continue to learn after you finish these pages!

A Note on Optimism

Many pages of this book will cover topics that have a darker edge. They offer perspective on the less positive aspects of non-binary existences. So, throughout this book when you feel slightly disheartened, I would urge you to adopt the practice of optimism. Optimism, according to the *Cambridge Dictionary*, is 'the quality of being full of hope and emphasizing the good parts of a situation, or a belief that something good will happen'. This is what you need to do for some sections of this book.

The role of this book is to help you and equip you with the knowledge to step into this world living your truth. So some parts have to share realities that are less than comfortable, but they will give you a better understanding of the world into which you step.

I hope that by using optimism as a tool to provide a positive outcome to my words, you will be able to help yourself be grounded in the world. It will also provide you with a path to follow to find better solutions for yourself.

If You're Reading This to Become a Better Ally

First of all, well done for taking this step to improve your under-standing of the intersections that exist in the world. As you read, many sections will be addressed to a non-binary reader, and I make no apology for not speaking directly to you, as there are millions of books that already do that. Instead, absorb how it feels to exist in a world that gives with one hand and takes with the other.

Some conversations may make you feel uncomfortable, and that is good thing. Through discomfort, real change occurs. I am not joking when I say that we so desperately need change in our favour. I didn't want you to feel completely left out, so there is a chapter that concerns you, Chapter 10, and this is the one I hope you take the most from, but each and every other chapter is just as vital for you to read.

Read the positives and the negatives, and all that lies between. My challenge to you, my darling ally, is to work out ways you can help us as a community. Become the ally we so desperately need. Then go about your life acting on those changes, holding other people with your privilege accountable and being a better human!

A Note on Cisgender

Cisgender refers to anyone who identifies with the gender they were assigned at birth, typically meaning male or female. This means that anyone who is happy with the gender they were assigned at birth, and does not feel the need to question it, is cisgender.

Some cisgender people are offended when they are referred to as cis by a non-cis person. They tend to shut down conversations before hearing out non-cis people, but that's their own business. Cisgender is not a slur – it is simply an easy term to use in a conversation or writing to convey gender identities.

Chapter 1

Who Are You?

So, reader, now that we are settled down with this book, I feel like I should congratulate you for choosing the guide you have in your hands. This definitely feels like the spiel you get when you buy a new appliance – 'Congratulations on your new purchase of a [insert generic electronic product that will have marginal success in your life here], read this section to set it up' – which it really isn't.

Whether you are exploring your gender for the first time or the hundred and first time, an ally in the making or a complete novice when it comes to the world of non-binary, welcome. This is a safe space, designed with a realistic but positive slant on the world in which we exist. It would be a disservice to you if I presented you a book full of 'positive vibes only'. Instead, it will be full of real human emotions because that is what life is about!

Who Am I?

This chapter is all about you, and mostly the rest of the book is too. It is helpful for you to get to know me a little better before I guide you through these pages. So, in a section all about you, spare a few pages for me!

I have long been a passionate lover of the French language. Now, that does not mean that I can 'parle français', and to be honest, darling, there is more chance of me becoming the next Pope than ever being fluent in French. One of the boundaries to my lack of any other languages but English is dyslexia. I struggled getting to grips with this initial language, so by the time modern European languages were on the curriculum for me there was no chance they would ever sink in.

I did, however, really love my French lessons! My brain knew it wasn't for me, so it let me relax, but also I behaved well enough to be placed in a class with children less likely to bully me. French lessons became something of a 'sanctuaire' for me. For any non-French speakers, this is what Demi Moore screamed in the terrifying Disney version of *The Hunchback of Notre Dame*, and it means 'sanctuary'. I can feel you getting restless, but don't worry, there is a point here!

My favourite French teacher was Madame Schwartzman. She hailed from Austria, so taught French and German, and was really, really lovely. We love a triple threat! She couldn't have been more than five feet tall, but she held a class's attention like no other. At the beginning of each lesson, she would charge into the classroom and begin a barrage of fluent French that melted the inside of my brain. I knew that I was supposed to understand what was being said to me, but I don't think I mastered the stunning prose of 'Je joue au ping-pong' until much later, and thus I sat in a perfect French daze.

Once the objectives were set, and register had been taken, the divine Madame Schwartzman would then repeat her stunning French monologue in plain English and all would become clear. This is how I felt when I realized I was non-binary. I knew that I didn't feel at home in the binary options of gender presented to me, but I had no idea what any of the language being used meant. I had no idea what pronouns to use. I didn't know how to explain any of it. My brain melted in a very similar way.

There is a maelstrom of information and expectations placed on the wider transgender community, but a lot of heat is felt within the non-binary community. This external pressure can feel as confusing as the first ten minutes of Madame Schwartzman's French lessons.

Only with time and after having it explained to me from various outlets of information did I slowly work out how I felt. I started the journey of working out what it meant to be me. This isn't a 'snap your fingers' affair. I am no Mary Poppins, darling, but I will guide you in a similar way to Madame Schwartzman, and because you are reading my words, we can take this as gently as you like – after all, this is your time with my words.

What Is Non-Binary?

I've been told many times that to know a concrete definition for non-binary would be helpful. This is for many reasons, most of which I will explore with you in the following pages. I must say, however, that to define non-binary beyond a personal level is to try to catch smoke with one's bare hands: impossible and a highly silly way to waste a Wednesday afternoon.

I can give you my personal experience. I do so not for allies but for my non-binary angels reading, as some part of this explanation may resonate, affirm or perhaps set you on a path of personal exploration.

Humans are visual beings. Gender is easy to imagine as colours. Male can be seen as blue and female as pink. Many people assume incorrectly that non-binary is purple – a blend of two gender identities. I don't know about you, but my gender identity is not Tinky Winky from the Teletubbies!

Non-binary exists on a sliding scale with 'typical assumed' male and female identifiers at either end. A non-binary person is any combination of colours on that scale, up, down and all around. There is no fixed point for any of us, and it is not a linear affair. This is why non-binary as a term is so wonderfully accessible. It doesn't constrain us or require us to be at a fixed point on that scale. It can be confusing to wrap your head around this if you are new to this subject, especially when many of us have grown up in a world fixed by binary expectations of gender, but it is simple. Non-binary is not fixed and has no expectations. The freedom the term brings to our identity is so wonderful because it just makes sense for so many of us.

I can tell you that all non-binary people interact with what it means to be them in very different ways, and to assume we're all the same is a rather large oversight. Think about roses. Would you presume that they are all the same? The internet helpfully informs me that there are over 200 different types of roses, and just like roses, non-binary people are a beauty to behold. We may have similarities, but we are not identical in any way.

Perhaps the very nature of our fluid being renders a definition of our identity quite pointless. To try and hem us in with a set of rules and guidelines is to refute the very existence of non-binary. In trying to understand us, you have erased us. After all, spending so much time trying to ascertain just which type of rose is in front of you means that you will miss the beauty of it blooming.

Instead, I say this to you: if you're an ally, don't worry about defining who we are. We know who we are or are on the path to working that out. Instead, why don't you worry about who you are? See how far you get when we ask you to succinctly describe your gender identity in under two minutes...

Genderqueer, Gender Diverse, Non-Binary, Queer

Terms and labels are something of a sticking point in the community. For some, labels are very defining and helpful, giving clear and distinctive parameters to their identity. Other people find them to be restrictive and go for looser terms that help them explain their gender identity in a way that is not fixed.

Non-binary for some, is looser terminology, but for others, feels restrictive. Genderqueer is a term that can be used by non-binary people, but also those who do not identify with any label at all. The fluidity of some terms is helpful for many as it leaves the interpretation up to the individual.

If you are trying to work out the language you use to refer to yourself and your gender identity, practise what feels comfortable for you by looking at each term and seeing which fits. This is a process that can take time, and that's okay. Below I have broken down some key terms or ways to refer to yourself to help you.

- **Transgender**
  It is helpful to think of transgender as an umbrella term for anyone who is not comfortable with the gender they were assigned at birth. This includes people who transition, but transgender (and trans as a shorter term) does not necessarily mean a transition has to take place. Non-binary people can also refer to themselves as trans, but some don't use this term.

- **Non-binary**
  This refutes the binary options of male and female, and allows the identifier to exist neutrally, blend gender identities or anything in between. It is also important to note that people who have transitioned can identity as non-binary too.

- **Agender**

  The 'a' here means without, so agender people are without gender and express that however they want. This can take the form of androgynous, super femme or even masc energy – it is always individual.

- **Genderqueer**

  This is similar to agender, non-binary and other terms such as gender diverse. Genderqueer is a term for those who refute gender binaries and norms, mixing gender identities, and allows them to self-determine their gender identity.

Understanding that there is no one way to define yourself, and knowing that there can be interactions, similarities and crossovers with so many of these terms, should help you begin to understand your own gender identity a bit more. It is also helpful for those who feel settled in their terminology: reading through this list, they may find a better fit. That is great. Be open to changes happening over time because our gender identities evolve with us.

So Why Is Your Gender Identity Amazing?

Put simply, seeing a world beyond binaries is one of the most freeing things because it removes any preordained decisions or expectations from your life. This sounds dramatic, but, if you think back to your past, so much of what has been expected of you has been down to a yes or no answer. This has left no room for the nuanced nature of human difference that exists in all of us.

Taking the first steps outside this traditional approach to life can feel very tough. Although you have made some great realizations within yourself, the world has yet to move with you. A simplistic approach would suggest that our lives are destined only to be tough, but with some thought it is a far brighter picture.

Essentially, you hold a secret: one of the best ways to live your life is to march to the beat of your own drum. There are no rules. We have set our own rules about what we do and don't want to express. Our gender is the reflection of that. In short, we are the most authentic we can be because we have transcended the restraints of binary gender.

Who Do You Think You Are?

Unlike cisgender people, we get to ask ourselves 'Who do we think we are?' This question allows us to work out what our lives could look like if we begin to act in a manner that nourishes our truth. This might sound so at odds with everything you have heard up until now, but, in putting ourselves first, we honour the past struggles we have gone through. We provide ourselves with a level of clarity many never achieve. This is not a straightforward process. You shouldn't imagine that this is something you can tick off your to-do list tomorrow afternoon.

Holding space is a concept that I was introduced to by the amazing life coach Char Bailey. In the context in which she used it, it meant to hold time for others who needed it. I would like to adapt this and suggest that we can also hold space for ourselves. As we acknowledge that our self-development is something we need to allot time to, in holding space, we set no alarms, deadlines or expectations!

This is a form of self-love, compassion or even just a way to reduce pressure in a life that can feel very intense. No one's identity has to be ready to go after two minutes. After all, we're not microwavable rice.

'Self-Love' or 'Selflessness'

Personal joy is something we are seeking in these pages, and we need to work out how to unlock that potential. *Death Becomes Her* is a fantastic film, and, to this day, watching it is one of the best ways to spend an afternoon in my opinion, even if my own mother disagrees with me. In this instance I feel confident enough to say she is wrong!

I hope this is a relevant reference to you; if not, please go and watch this cinematic masterpiece immediately. I'm sure you are wondering what this has got to do with this book – well, stick with me on this one. Meryl Streep sizzles as the somewhat wilted, self-devoted Madeline Ashton, who to me has always had an overlooked charm and a gravitational pull like no other fictional character. In the opening scene, Ashton performs her one-woman show, and sings the rather narcissistic masterpiece 'I see me'.

The lyrics are an ode to her sense of self-importance, with Ashton describing herself as an 'actress', 'star', 'sweetheart', 'temptress' and 'dream of others' among other things (watch the film for the full effect).

I'm not, of course, encouraging you to steal Goldie Hawn's fiancé, or search for an elixir of eternal life (however, if this is your raison d'être, you have my blessing, I won't stand in your way). But there is something in this opening scene that can be used when it comes to asserting your right to personal joy.

Many of us have languished under the false premise that we are somehow wrong, broken or less deserving. Yet we find ourselves and own our unique nature uninhibited by binaries. Suddenly it all falls into place. The possibility of life opens itself up to you, and there are no barriers. This is a process lovingly called finding yourself, and in essence is years and years of struggle and a life half lived, until the moment when you uncover your true identity.

However, many of us are left as our only cheerleader, and we have to nourish our sense of self alone. This cannot be done half-heartedly – it requires a true belief in who we are, otherwise the fight has all been a wasted enterprise.

I have totally hijacked Robert Zemeckis's black comedy for

my own purposes, but I believe in some small way we owe it to ourselves to be in love with who we are. Life is really hard, and it would be harder if we weren't devoted to ourselves. It may be that writing this book has gone to my head, but I urge you to take a leaf out of Ms Ashton's book and treat yourself to a little self-obsession.

Being selfish is not a very popular approach to life, but I would argue as non-binary people we owe it to ourselves to be selfish and treat life as an opportunity for pleasure. The structures in our society, and indeed the opinions of oppressors (actual or complicit), leave very little space for marginalized communities. Our sense of self can feel very cramped. If we assert our right to self-appreciation and in a sense become a touch more like Madeline Ashton and enjoy some selfish indulgence, then this is the route to more joy in our lives.

'Selfish' is used here in a way that many ignore because it takes more energy to understand that there are layers of selfishness. For many, selfishness as an emotional state is very cut and dried; however, there is nuance to the conversation surrounding acts of selfishness. Politicians are selfish in a way that causes harm to others, but we as non-binary people are not harming anyone else by putting ourselves first. Even if we were politicians – imagine that – we would still be able to put the needs of hungry children first; I'm looking at you, Conservatives.

Our act of selfishness is actually closer to selflessness, because all we are doing is holding space for ourselves and caring for our sense of self. This is no bad thing, and you need to hear that, so I will say it again: it is not selfish to be selfish when it comes to loving yourself first and foremost.

The Queer Culture Gap

One of the issues that has hindered personal growth for the LG-BTQIA+ community is the society and wider world that we live in. The things surrounding us don't match how we feel. This is what I have coined the Queer Culture Gap. I know, very clever! This is essentially the time lag where we have moved to a new point of freedom and development with our identities; however, culture and society have yet to catch up.

The space and time from you feeling you could be non-binary to feeling fully affirmed as a non-binary person is a large and gaping chasm. Nice, right? This is the same for many forms of identity, sexuality and gender. We're not alone in feeling very lost and vulnerable. One of my deepest wishes is that the pages of this book can be a comforting companion on your journey of self-discovery, while society does the work to catch up to us.

It is all well and good saying that there are shoots of representation in social media, on television and in literature. There is a lot that does not match up with how we feel and that can limit our growth, making us feel like a sunflower in the shade. A moment of darkness in this opening chapter is here to remind you that so much of how we're made to feel as a community is not within our control.

How Representation Has Held You Back

Representation is really important when it comes to affirming feelings and questions we have about our mind, body and identity. Representation can hold us back. To be precise, it is the lack of representation that has held us back.

Non-binary was just a word to me until I saw someone who

was gender diverse. What was so different to the sliver of trans and gender non-comforting representation that we see in the media was that this person was *happy*. Honestly this small chink of light in a cloudy sky is the one thing that kick-started my own journey of self-discovery when I was in my early twenties.

This is another layer of responsibility that is not yours but is still placed on your shoulders, and then you are left alone to deal with the consequences. It is so easy to see why the majority of cishet white people thrive in their lives because it is easy to see how to live like that. They are surrounded by representation, which gives them tips and reassurance that they are valid.

We are already playing at a disadvantage. Imagine you are going to play a ping-pong match, and you have practised extensively, but when you get there, you find you don't have a bat. You have to play with your hands, and of course your opponent beats you at every turn. This is what it is like to live with no representation to validate your identity. Frustrating is an understatement...

The Only Way Is Up

There is a silver lining, and a big one at that. Put simply, things can only get better. I sincerely believe that to be true. There are more and more allies who are waking up to the idea that there are an infinite number of ways to live your life. Representation is on the rise!

I can give you clear examples. I would not have been writing this book ten years ago, but now brands, publishers and household names are putting their weight behind trans and gender non-conforming people. For the first time ever the playing field is scheduled to be levelled.

Now, like all improvements, this will take time. I remember

when I was a child, the heady anticipation of snow, and hoping night after night that I would wake up and open the curtains to a thick, school-closing blanket of snow. Nine times out of ten this never happened. Yet there were occasions when my wishes were granted, and just like snow, you will one day see a massive change that you never thought possible. This is a joyous thing to behold. In the words of 1980s pop sensation Yazz, 'The only way is up, baby'!

Life Is Short

This may be a shocking statement for you to see in a book that is supposed to help you, but please allow me to explain myself. As I explored earlier, some of the changes we hope to see in society will take time. We can all agree on that. In the meantime, are we supposed to sit and twiddle our thumbs?

Well, in short, no! I want you to see the nuanced conversation that is taking place here. The environment that exists in our society may not feel like the most comfortable one for non-binary people, and you would be right in thinking that. It may never be fully accommodating to us, but we cannot wait our whole lives for this to happen.

There is also the chance that by accepting who you are right now, and embracing that in all aspects of your life, you yourself will play a vital role in visibility. Presenting as your true self will help the next generations and create ripples of change in the pond of life. Never wait for things to happen to you, darling. The time is now. Go out and live your life. It will be so worth it!

Key Takeaways from This Chapter

- ♥ Your gender identity may not make sense at first, and that is okay.
- ♥ There is no one way to be non-binary!
- ♥ We're like roses; each one of us is an individualistic beauty.
- ♥ There are a plethora of labels; it is okay to be confused.
- ♥ Leaning into your gender identity is true authenticity and will set you free.
- ♥ You are not microwavable rice; your sense of self cannot be rushed!
- ♥ You deserve to be selfish in the pursuit of pleasure.

Chapter 1, Over and Out

So that was your first chapter. How did you find it?

There was a lot of information on those pages and, as a reader myself, I sometimes find books that provide a lot of information to be overwhelming. How does one remember all the things being said? Non-fiction burnout is a real thing. Hopefully, this is something we can overcome in this book together.

As you move through the book, there will be things that I refer back to, but also there will be small prompts and reminders where you might need them. Think of my words as a companion that you can rely upon. There is no instantaneous fix required, and certainly no quizzes, or maybe there are.*

So take a deep breath and relax into these pages. You don't need to remember my words off by heart. Instead, know you can come back to my words time and time again; that's what they are here for. Okay, my darlings, turn the page and delve into Chapter 2...

* There aren't, I promise!

Chapter 2

The Obsession with Gender

One of the biggest hurdles for us as non-binary people is other people. Now, for some naysayers, this is us shifting the blame onto others, but trust me, other people and our society have a lot to answer for. We are often the focus of media debates, rubbish articles in newspapers and indirect attacks on Twitter.

It saddens me to write this, but due to a lack of understanding, and natural human laziness, we are seen as a topic and not as people. I am convinced that cisgender people are more obsessed with our gender identities than we are, and I am sure you will have had similar experiences.

The Reason Our Gender Identity Matters So Much

As non-binary people, we spend so much time explaining our gender identity to other people. This is not for our benefit. One of the reasons we are held back in life is because cisgender people are fascinated by us, but they see us as a novelty and forget to treat us like the people we are.

You see, the idea of having the confidence to go against the preordained examples of gender that have existed for hundreds of thousands of years frightens people. We are seen as otherworldly because we have chosen to eschew tradition and patriarchal presets in favour of a life lived for ourselves. It is laughable but it is one of the biggest reasons our lives are so hard.

Throughout history anyone considered outside the parameters of 'normal' has been viewed as entertainment or, at worst, a physical threat to the safety of others. Witch-hunts were the favourite way to rid the world of people who challenged the status quo, with wise women and social outcasts singled out and persecuted. Although many were charged, the legitimacy of most charges was questionable and essentially showed society's biggest weakness – fear of individual power. A far less fatal, but just as brutally cruel, example comes from the mid-sixteenth century onwards when circuses ran sideshows that showcased people who had biological anomalies. Thankfully these merciless cruelties are no longer in operation.

Now the show has moved online. Articles written by questionable sources attack the LGBTQIA+ community and present *us* as the new biological anomalies. So, as much as your gender identity is important to who you are, it will never be as important as it is to strangers who are threatened and fascinated by you.

Human curiosity is a feature of life, but when you understand where the pressure comes from, it feels far less personal. We are the current centre of attention. Pretty soon, something else will grab the mainstream's attention, and we will be left in peace. Won't that be wonderful?!

Pronouns

Pronouns are the site of many a gender battle. If they signposted the places where these battles take place, we would forever be tripping over blue plaques and brown road signs. For years the conversation around pronouns has been centred on the gender diverse and our need to be pleased.

This is here for a few reasons. First, most people have never suffered the searing pain of being misgendered on a daily basis. Second, most people assume that the work surrounding pronouns should be done by those who use pronouns that sit outside of the binary. Both of these incorrect and unfair issues are big hurdles.

Recently I had the misfortune of sitting through a meeting where another person steered the conversation away from the topic (gender neutral cosmetic enhancements) to steamroll everyone with his opinion that pronouns in email bios were pointless and made him feel uncomfortable.

Here is the learning point for allies. If everyone put their pronouns in communiqués and in social media bios, regardless of gender identity, those who are gender diverse would have some of the pressure lifted from their shoulders. This is the conversation that needs to take place. Its importance should never be downplayed. However, it's a small piece of a larger puzzle, and there is much more allies need to be talking about.

What Is Hegemony?

Society has a great influence on the subjects that reside in its systems, and this is kept in check by hegemony. Hegemony ensures that the ideals of society are seen as the most beneficial to the economic, political and governing wellbeing of the state.

This means certain characteristics are favoured by society. These are seen as the mainstream 'ideals'. Thus, those of us who exist outside of this are seen as a threat to the stability of society. This huge factor is why we face so much backlash.

Why Society Is Fuelled by Stereotypes

Stereotypes are not good things. I want to be upfront with you here.

As humans we all use them. It is a big part of being human. I owe everything I know about stereotypes to renowned sociologist and cultural theorist Stuart Hall, who wrote at length about their uses in human life. I will give you the CliffsNotes for ease!

Stereotypes are used in our brains to understand the people we meet in our lifetime. They are generalizations about others – assumptions that put people into categories. This is a time-saving device used to store information. It allows us to keep ourselves at the forefront of our thinking.

Checkboxes

One of the main barriers to enjoying being yourself in our society is the issues that checkboxes can throw up. Other people will use checkboxes to categorize you, and society will also use them against you too. Checkboxes act as a very efficient and quick filtering system that strips personal variations away from people. They allow society to see people as data. How lovely and dehumanizing.

All humans, even gender diverse people, use this system to quickly file away information we know about people. We can work out where to place them in our lives, relying heavily on the aforementioned stereotyping. When it comes to filing away non-binary people, we suddenly have a big question mark over our heads. This is another example of the problems we face in our life being perpetuated by other people.

What Is Heteronormativity?

Heteronormative behaviour clings to the binary view of the world, by working to assert that the best way to approach life is with male or female as the only options. This covers gender, alignment of biological gender, sexuality and physical relationships with other bodies.

This sounds bad, but when you think about it, it's worse! Conformity to heteronormative demands has damaging effects, as it restricts and ignores the nuanced existences of millions of gender diverse people. It permeates into society through media, viewpoints and politics. It is perpetuated by a lack of diversity in company hiring, governance of the country and a failure to be inclusive across many levels. It interacts dangerously with terms like tradition and moral values, as it suggests that those who go against heteronormative behaviour are creating trouble or are somehow deviant.

A clear example of this comes from the world's biggest news cooperation, the BBC. When it airs programmes that include a conversation about transgender people, particularly trans women, the BBC insists that a cisgender woman has to be present in this conversation in order to safeguard the rights of cisgender women. This ignores the difficulties and hardships of being trans, and is a classic example of heteronormative favouritism. There is no place for this kind of behaviour in our society, and with time it will fade, but it requires the work of allies to erase it fully.

Why Stereotypes Don't Work for Non-Binary People

Stereotypes don't work for non-binary people because for many people we meet in our lifetime, this may be their first interaction with, or knowledge about non-binary gender identities. Suddenly, there is no box to file us in. We cause consternation because we take focus away from their brain's typical selfish default.

While this is clearly the fault of poor diversity and representation in the world around us, it somehow falls to us to educate and navigate the bluster of others who treat us as liars. I want you to know you don't have to be an educator. Google exists for all these questions. Others need to do better for us and educate themselves.

Why Non-Binary Identities Scare People

We aren't easy to understand immediately because we don't offer a yes or no answer. We require more effort to be understood. Humans are lazy. Our identities can quickly cause conflict. You need to remember that this is not on you and isn't something you should be trying to fix.

Our identity is seen as novel or new, but you and I both know how ridiculous this is. Never forget that! We spend a lot of time dealing with other people's emotions, and not living our lives. Instead, we should focus on ourselves and prioritize our own pleasure.

Your Gender Identity Doesn't Matter

It may come as a shock to hear this, but your gender identity doesn't matter. You have come to find who you are over time. It is something that will continue to develop as you move through life. You have done it. The more time we focus on our gender identity, the less time we spend time *actually living*.

We spend too much time focusing on people's gender and not enough time focusing on actual people. Sometimes we need an example to follow. If we focus more on who we are, and less on what category we fit into, over time we will change this discourse.

We will never forget who we are. That personal growth can continue to nourish our souls, but we are so much more than a label. I want to hear about non-binary people doing amazing things because they are amazing people, and not just because they are non-binary. This starts with us, and we have the power to shift the focus of the conversation.

The Trend Argument

'Oh but non-binary is just a trend.'
'This is just a phase; you'll grow out of it eventually.'

These are just a couple of examples of comments I am sure you will have heard. They are exhausting. I could delve into historical examples of gender variations, bring you chapters on genderless communities in South Asia, two-spirit individuals in Indigenous

American communities, a recognized third gender in Samoan culture and examples of acceptance of gender diversity in eighteenth-century Italy or the Māhū of Hawaii. However, this book is not about proving we exist. We don't need to do that. We know it! Comments and conversations like this erode some of the happiness we have found in being our true selves.

However, there is a simple and clear way to undermine these responses to your existence. The twenty-first century is responsible for so many things. One of those is the advent of the internet. The problem child is the smartphone. Most of us have access to a device or two at all times. Suddenly, the whole world is at our fingertips. This provides a constant stream of words, images and videos. We can see more of it now than has ever been possible before. So now gender identities are also far more visible. Non-binary naysayers are confused by this new visibility. We have always existed, Carol. It just hasn't always been so easy to see us. We're not a trend. We are finally getting the visibility we deserve.

♥ ♥ ♥

We talk about non-binary representation, but part of me wishes it wasn't an issue. I love wrestling, I love music, there is so much that I love besides just being non-binary. Ask me about that! On the other hand, it becomes this thing where, if people don't ask me about it, they're going to get it from the media, which is usually written by cisgender people who don't have a clue. We're at a very surface-level understanding of queerness right now, because journalism is such a tick-box world.

I feel like companies are trying to keep up with us because they want our money. Companies do more harm than good. They launch 70 different gender options or whatever it is as a performative gesture, and then we have to deal with the media fallout. News outlets, brands, corporations and companies give us a crumb, and then the media turns around and says that's what we've been fighting for, so it makes our activism look superficial. We get the tiniest bit of progress — like the non-binary icon Mx Potato Head — and then it looks like what we've been asking for.

In reality, we're asking not to be harassed. We're asking to be understood. We're asking for better representation. Yet companies give us these crumbs, voluntarily, because they want to profit from us. Thanks for the crumbs I guess, but nobody cared!

♥ ♥ ♥

Jake Hall *(they/them), journalist*

What Could Change to Make Non-Binary People's Lives Easier?

The easiest way to change all of this mess, and make our lives easier as non-binary people is simple. We need to be seen as human beings, not as a problem! We are not responsible for the confusion of others. It is not our fault that gender identities outside the binary are not taught to everyone.

We are given an unfair disadvantage in life because currently we are being *talked about* and not being *talked to*. How can anyone understand all our facets as humans if we are not listened to? It is an impossible task to understand everybody you meet, but we should be given a chance. If we meet people who don't have the experience to understand who we are, why do we have to be on the back foot? Why do we have to go to extreme lengths to prove that we do exist?

One of the biggest challenges that non-binary people face is that we are not shown the basic human decency of respect. Cisgender identities have existed for as long as non-binary identities have, yet there is far more acceptance of the former. We do not exist to prove a point that binary identities are wrong. Cisgender people should show us the basic respect we are asking for!

Key Takeaways from This Chapter

- ♥ The discourse surrounding non-binary people does not exist within us. It exists as a response to our assertive pleasure in being who we are.
- ♥ We are not to blame and should never change who we are to please others.

- ♥ Hegemonic bias means the lives of minorities are not prioritized – yet another factor outside of our control.
- ♥ Stereotypes are a currency of society but do not apply to
everybody. They have a dehumanizing effect.
- ♥ Repeat after me: 'My identity is not a trend or a phase.' It
never will be.
- ♥ We are not novel or new. The advances in media only make
it seem this way. Remember, correlation does not imply
causation!
- ♥ To move on from the 'us versus them' argument, we need to
be treated like humans and to be shown the respect we truly
deserve.

Chapter 3

Understanding Your Past

Dealing with other people is one thing, but we also have to admit that we carry baggage from our past that affects us daily. Similar to other people's obsession with our gender identity, this is not our fault, but if we fail to acknowledge it, it can control us.

Growing up is a tough process for everyone, but as non-binary people, I would argue we have to contend with another layer of complexity. I am not here to dredge up bad memories. I do not want to cause emotional angst. The next few pages are here to help you change the way you see things for the better.

What Is Trauma?

Trauma is an odd term because it has many connotations. Many people think that its only application is to the most severe experiences. Trauma occurs when an event places a person under pressure and leaves them changed.

Trauma can be caused by a horrific customer service experience, accidental consumption of a snail found in a pot of jam or verbal attacks. Trauma is a result of these experiences. We carry this around with us, after the event.

As non-binary people, we all have trauma that we take into our endeavours. For so many of us, it is the way we have been treated in the past that affects how we treat ourselves right now! This is nothing new. I am sure it doesn't surprise you, but, left unchecked, that trauma can have a continuous negative impact on your wellbeing.

Trauma isn't something we deserve. Like so many of the negative aspects of our life as non-binary people, it has been done to us without consent. We have to work out how to move on with our lives, and without understanding what trauma truly is, we are not in control of it.

What Is Intersectionality?

Intersectionality is considering all the different intersections of discrimination that may hold a person back and how, combined, they compound the individual effects. This looks across all minority groups, and brings into consideration layers of privilege and comfort in society.

Intersectionality was coined by black feminist Kimberlé Crenshaw, who identified that the experience of black women could not be understood as just being a woman or being black. Instead we must investigate the relationship between both.

It is about including and centring on the voices of those who have been oppressed by social situations and ensuring that help is not just aimed at white, masculine or heterosexual experiences. Equality without intersectionality helps only the least oppressed in society. Being aware of your own intersections will also help you better understand some of your past traumas in a better way.

Fight or Flight

Fight or flight is a very simple concept. It makes most of our decisions for us, without us even knowing it. In its simplest form, fight or flight is a physiological response to a perceived threat or harmful event. A hundred thousand years ago, our ancestors will have used this to evaluate situations that were life or death scenarios. Their response would either ensure their survival or would erase them from prehistoric timelines.

Fast forward to today, and as I'm sure you will have noticed, we no longer have to hunt to survive, and Google has made it very easy to ascertain whether certain berries will be harmful or not. However, while the most essential uses for fight or flight have faded from our lives, the instinct is still present. It is the number one cause of conflict for anyone perceived as 'different'.

Non-binary people are clear and easy targets, which fills me with sadness to write, but it is an irrefutable part of who we are. We cannot erase what has been done to us. To try would be far more damaging than reliving those experiences afresh. Understanding the reasons why can make it easier to deal with. We can see how it wasn't as personal as it felt at the time.

You Have Already Beaten Your Bullies

We all have memories of school that send shivers down our spines and I don't want to make you revisit them. However, I would like to remind you that you picked this book up. It is unapologetically about you choosing to love your life completely. You are in a place of learning and self-growth. You have grown beyond the reach of bullies and past trauma.

You have come so far. Growth can be painful, and a long process, but you are here. That is a massive achievement. I still recoil at the memories of my bullies, but I know I have grown, and that is something to be proud of!

No matter where you are on your journey of self-acceptance and love, every day is an achievement. You must always remember this. Your trauma is not ruling you. You have chosen you. That is such an important part of loving yourself.

How to Move on from Trauma

Trauma at its core is traumatic. No surprises there! It can dominate the narratives we hold about ourselves. With some simple shifts, we can change a key theme of our narrative. We are victims of abusive behaviour – that is a given – but we are not powerless.

We have had the opportunity to see some of the worst human behaviour, but we know how to avoid it, and what situations make it more likely. This allows us to create some safety barriers to prevent future trauma.

One sure-fire fact that should bolster your security in choosing a positive outlook on the future is that we never have to go backwards. One of the basic inevitabilities of life is that time will always march forwards.

I can't rule out future circumstances that will cause trauma, but I can say with certainty you will be in a better place to process and understand the event that you experienced, and it will not become a life-altering chapter – more of a bad day in a sea of much better days.

Past Trauma = Future Understanding

Knowing what caused trauma is one thing, but knowing what you can do with it is a completely separate thing altogether. I get asked one question a lot: 'If you could change your past, would you erase your bullies?' I know the interviewer wants me to say 'Yes', but that is not my answer.

I am not grateful for my past trauma. No one deserves to be treated like that, but without those events, you wouldn't be reading these words. The things we have been through offer us a chance to see the world from a different perspective.

Once you see the possibility that your past trauma can offer you future understanding, suddenly there is some purpose to your past pain.

The Power of Empathy

There is no denying that trauma will have caused damage that will result in fear, which is understandable. This shouldn't be an emotional response that stops you moving forwards. You are not the same person who went through those things. Do not expect your life to develop the same way.

Past experiences can become your strength and offer you a Rolodex of advice you can offer yourself and those around you. You have been through a lot. We all have. Now you are in the unique position to transcend the bad past experiences and help yourself, and others, deal with similar issues in the future.

Empathy is a superpower. It is a passive product of trauma. You can relate to people with similar experiences and help them come to terms with it in a compassionate way. If government officials had one per cent of the empathy the non-binary community have, the world would be a very different place.

Using Compassion as Currency

Empathy is an emotional response and is wonderful, but alone can only go so far. However, it can be actioned further. This is unlocked with the power of compassion. Compassion is typically seen as the drive to help others, but in this context compassion is a personal pursuit.

Have compassion for your past. Make self-pleasure and personal appreciation the centre of your self-development. This kind of compassion doesn't need grand gestures or actions. Instead, it thrives on visibility and relatability.

There is a massive amount of power in you owning and appreciating your existence in a way that to many may look selfish, but we know we truly deserve. It can be hard to love yourself when the world hasn't always shown you the love you need. We don't need to wait for them to appreciate us, to love ourselves. Instead, use the empathy and compassion from your past experiences to strengthen the bond you have with your sense of self. Use it as a currency for a more enjoyable life.

♥ ♥ ♥

We do so much as a community to help and care for others. Every non-binary person I know online is engaging in work that helps people to connect in a world that can feel like it is on fire. Non-binary creators are full of empathy and love for others. Having empathy for ourselves is walking away when someone is crossing lines. I like to see non-binary people taking the time to have empathy for themselves.

I've learned so much about my own sense of empathy in the past few years. Empathy is one of my defining characteristics because of my grandmother – who was a community nurse for 40 years and a priest in her later years. She was a very important person to me – she taught me to try to see love in all people. I keep that alive in myself and in my artwork.

I fully believe that community care is empathy. Whether that is donating to mutual aid, creating for others or starting a local community group, empathy has been the root of everything I do.

♥ ♥ ♥

Wednesday Holmes (they/them), artist

The Power of Self-Sabotage

Other people are not the only ones to have caused us issues. We are also part of the problem. I'm talking about something within all of us – our internal voice! This voice can be just as damaging as the people that have caused us the greatest pain.

That internal voice can pull us lower than we have ever been in our darkest moments, but what's crazy is that that internal voice is powered by our brain. Our lowest moments are compounded, filed, saved and remembered by our brain, and easily retrieved at moments when we really don't need them!

Our inner saboteur is never far from the surface. It has an annoying habit of ruining really good days. Understanding trauma – in the sense that it can't be changed but that your understanding of it can be changed – can do wonders when it comes to tackling your inner saboteur.

I can't change what people in your past have done to you, but I can stop you being prone to self-sabotage. Not a single one of you reading this can honestly say you haven't self-sabotaged in your past. It is part of owning the flawed beings we all are.

So how can you move forwards the minute you put this book down? Well, you have the option just not to act on what your brain is piping into your head. If you like underlining things in books, then this would be a good part to underline. Don't listen to those silky lies, and move your headspace into a different mode that understands your brain has these thoughts by default, but they have no consequence on how much you are going to enjoy your day.

Never forget that you are in charge!

Key Takeaways from This Chapter

- ♥ Trauma isn't something we deserve.
- ♥ Being aware of your own intersections will help you better understand some of your past traumas.
- ♥ You have come so far!
- ♥ Trauma can offer you future understanding.
- ♥ Fear is normal, but it shouldn't rule you.
- ♥ Empathy can help you love yourself more.
- ♥ Remember to ignore your inner saboteur.

Reclaiming Your Past

This section's main goal is to help you understand the subtext of your past and what it means for you right now. You don't have to do it all at once. This can be a gradual process.

To chart your progress and celebrate small wins, use this fun bingo sheet and start your journey to understand your past. All you need to do is cross off the squares as you understand and experience them in your life! The first with a full house (all boxes crossed) wins. Sorry, there are no cash prizes, darling!

Reclaiming your past BINGO

You remember your bullies, but they are not in control of you!	Words used against you no longer sting like they did before!	You know you cannot control your past and have moved forwards with this knowledge!
You hear your inner saboteur but no longer listen to its lies!	*Reclaiming your past*	You have reclaimed slurs like queer as positive descriptors!
You have converted your past pain into methods that are bringing you pleasure now!	You embrace new days as the positive fresh starts that they are!	You know your past doesn't define you but can help you enjoy your life right now!

Chapter 4

We're an Unfinished Novel

Metaphors are a big part of my writing. They allow an audience to consume a small parcel of information and digest it easily. Some metaphors are unhelpful, and some are incredibly useful. One of the most helpful I have found is the metaphor of your life being a novel.

This novel is full of your life. It has every detail up until this very moment. Yet, if you were to flick through the book, after today you would find empty pages. Your life is unfinished; the future pages are waiting to be written.

Join me as we explore a path not yet written, defining our own journeys...

Your Story Is Not Yet Finished

The best place to start is to allow this message to really sink in. We exist in a world that tries its hardest to move our existences to the sidelines of life. The media takes every opportunity to contest, speculate on and direct our very being. There is so much said about us that it can be hard to operate from our own knowledge of ourselves.

All of this accumulates in our psyche, and we hold this fallacy presented to us as some sort of prophetic plan of our lives to come. I don't know if you know how harmful this is, but it is incredibly damaging to your self-belief and vision of the future.

No one can accurately tell the future. As much as we would like to have that superpower, I don't think it will ever be a possibility. However, this leaves a lovely opening in our lives, and that is the wonder of endless possibilities. We know our journey and story up to this very moment. Beyond that – well, no one knows.

This means you have the ability and possibility to steer the course of your journey in any direction you want to. It may not be as simple as that day to day, but just knowing that all the future tomorrows are not planned, scripted or predestined should provide you with plenty of comfort.

You Have No Set Path

I alluded to a path not yet written. To some this may sound like an intangible nirvana of impossible iterations. Well, it is far more down to earth than that. This is not a soul-searching exercise requiring 37 years of silence. This is the simple concept that you can change what you are doing at any point.

This, in essence, means that you have the freedom to try all the things that are calling to you. Any burning desires can come to fruition if only you give them the space to do so. The magic of understanding that your path is not yet written is that it gives you comfort in taking the time you need to work things out at your own pace.

Forced rhubarb is one of the ways we get a seasonal product out of season, but rhubarb connoisseurs – they do exist, I checked – will always say that it is a very different thing when compared to natural rhubarb. So it is clear that forcing your existence through fear of changing your mind will create a different outcome.

Allowing yourself the space to take things one step at a time is a far healthier approach. It will allow you to figure how you feel one day at a time. You have nothing but time, my darling. This is the gift of being human. So take that and run with it.

Oh, and I despise all forms of rhubarb, so I can't tell you if there is a difference in the two types. You will have to work that out for yourself!

Family Dynamics

Families are hard. This is a facet of being human. However, this is heightened for gender diverse people. As we explore who we are, this begins to alter the information our families think they know about us. Tensions arise and tough conversations either cause conflict or don't take place at all, leaving a very large, queer elephant in the room.

The people we grow up around are supposed to act as the nourishing formula to create a well-rounded person. Society has suggested that their apparent maturity means they have authority when it comes to opinions and knowledge. As you mature, and from my own perspective, you find that this is not always the truth. Parents can love us but still harm us. This is just a fact.

Some non-binary people grow up with loving families who perhaps just don't understand them. Others grow up in fear. This is all tempered with thousands of experiences in between. Knowing how to spot harmful behaviour is very individual, and I can't give specific advice. However, I can say this: no one has the right to invalidate your experience and feelings. They cannot tell you how to be!

If a living situation becomes unsafe then please seek help. There is more advice at the end of this book should you need it.

What Is Microaggression?

Microaggression is a term first coined by Dr Chester Pierce, at Harvard in 1970. He said that microaggressions were 'subtle, stunning, often automatic, and non-verbal exchanges which are "put downs" of Blacks by offenders'.* We have seen this play out across many marginalized communities, and it is a reality for the queer community.

* Pierce, C., Carew, J., Pierce-Gonzalez, D. and Willis, D. (1978) 'An Experiment in Racism: TV Commercials.' In Pierce, C. (ed.) *Television and Education*. Beverly Hills, CA: Sage, p.65.

An example of a microaggression is a white person saying to a black person 'I'm not racist, I have black friends', which is essentially denying the existence of individual racism*. Another is a heterosexual person telling a homosexual person that they cannot be homophobic as they have gay friends. These are things people just should not say!

Microaggressions make day-to-day life harder. They prove that there are systematic failures in our society benefiting only the most privileged.

The Right Environment Is Key

I don't know if you grew any plants or vegetables when you were in your very first year of school, but we grew broad beans. This was to teach us about the life cycle of plants. One of the features I remember was ensuring the seeds had the perfect conditions to germinate, including light, moisture and warmth, otherwise the seed would never grow.

The environment we grow in is equally important and this goes beyond childhood to our whole life. You will know an environment is good for you if you're thriving. If not, work out how to make changes to help you grow. This could be by opening channels of dialogue with those that you live with, addressing the elephant in the room or by setting boundaries about the things you don't want to talk about. We all deserve to live our days in an environment that allows us to reach our full potential.

* If you want to explore more about microaggressions and race, Google 'systemic racism' to learn more about the racism that infects the very structure of our society.

What Is Gaslighting?

This is the action of making someone question their own thought process. Gaslighting is a form of emotional abuse. It creates an environment where doubt can blossom, causing so much damage. It can be overt or concealed, but it is very important to be aware of examples of gaslighting to ensure your own safety. These behaviours are big red flags, and they can come in many forms:

- **Diversion**
  This is the practice of changing the subject and moving a conversation away from the original discussion. This removes power and allows the gaslighter to control the discourse.

- **Withholding**
  This is essentially ignoring something and negating its existence: 'I don't know what you are talking about.'

- **Accusations of sensitivity**
  In trickier conversations, a gaslighting practitioner will accuse people of being overly sensitive. Terms like 'snowflake' can also be used in these circumstances.

- **Countering**
  This is a sneaky one because it brings in opinion, which people confuse with truth. Countering works by suggesting that your statement is not true, or that 'you have remembered that conversation incorrectly; that's not what I said/did/insinuated'.

Gaslighting is tricky because people who do it are very sensitive about being called out, especially when it is family. The best advice from my own experience is to limit interactions with someone who treats you like this.

The Control Is in Your Own Hands

There is a lot that you can control, and this obviously goes against the preset narratives that perhaps up until now have been presented to you. It is not a straightforward process. It is something that requires work on a regular basis. This may feel glum, but it is a fact of life for all people, not just our community.

There is plenty of room for diverse gender identities to coexist under the same roof, but this requires compromise on both sides. We discussed earlier how many of the issues we face are rooted in other people's emotions and issues, and this is the case here, yet again.

For those of you who are currently in an environment that is preventing you from flourishing, you have to work out how to soothe the fear in others. For many reasonable loving families, this can take the form of an open conversation that assuages fears on both sides. If you feel safe enough to discuss this with those around you, I would really encourage that.

However, I am aware that not all family dynamics are this safe. Compromise is key here! This may sound like a massive revision of a stand point, but we all have to pick our battles, and home is not one of them. The figures for LGBTQIA+ homelessness are stark, with 25 per cent of all homeless people coming from our community.

Such are the issues we face that, in these circumstances, compromising on certain issues can help keep you safe. Perhaps the discussions you have will take shape in a much slower format. You could tackle one person at a time, and if you have someone that you are closer to, allow them in to help you to approach the trickier family members.

It is also important to remember that this is never going to be a quick fix. Many people in similar situations to you will also be making slow but steady progress, making their living situation as comfortable as possible. There are resources at the end of this book that can help you if conversations with your family break down.

Find Your Own Family

In those instances where you can't have the conversations you need to have, the opportunity to turn to chosen family is one we must take. Chosen family can be anyone – friends, allies and support systems – that becomes a defining force in your life.

These are the relationships that I have found to be the most helpful in getting through the tough conversations I wished I could have had with family members. Your chosen family can be the ones you have the heart to hearts with, share the frustrations with and fill the gaps that having to make compromises can cause.

Those relationships are *so* important. I cannot urge you enough to forge your own chosen family even if your home situation is better than most. Having someone outside the four walls that you call home means that you always have someone on your side. There is someone to provide you with unbiased advice and, if you need it, a shoulder to cry on.

My chosen family is small, but the calls we share put my world to rights. They have brought me out of dark days and been there to celebrate my success. Never underestimate the necessity of chosen family.

A Note on Safe Spaces

A safe space is something you probably know of, but perhaps may not have experienced too much. We think of safe space in our society as places where minority groups can feel safe. In terms of our community we would assume a safe space to be a queer haven.

Yet many of us experience spaces that are less than safe daily. This is a realistic aspect of who we are and is defined by the violent opinions of others. Any space that makes you feel less than safe is not somewhere you should be. For some of us this is possible to navigate, but for others it isn't, with home life and family connections proving tricky.

This is why there is a need for digital communities to create safe spaces for people to access when they need – whether this be content, helplines, friendship groups, books like this and so many more. Safe spaces are not a given. Until that is the case, there is work to be done. If you're an ally reading this, this is for you to act upon!

The Finality of Friendship

Friendships can be tricky. Like all human relationships, they have their ups and downs. When we strike up these relationships, they feel unbreakable. Nothing could ever stop you from enjoying each other's company. Sadly, life gets in the way and you can drift apart, or small issues begin to rock the boat and the relationship begins to crumble.

Relationships are all two-way streets. You should both benefit from the interaction, and just as our chosen family can be our saviour, sometimes we need to see that some people are not meant to be. I recently heard someone say that some friendships have a time limit. They run their course, and when you know this has happened it is good to move on.

The hard thing for us is that these may be some of the first true friendships we have had as 'ourselves'. It is never a bad thing to put yourself first. So, if a relationship isn't working, don't suffer in silence for the good of the other person.

From experience, it is good to have closure. Have a frank and honest conversation about the situation. For the other person to remove you from their life abruptly would be very hard to deal with, so I wouldn't suggest you act in this manner either. Treat them with the respect that you would imagine you yourself would deserve. People come and go, but you are a constant in your own life, so make sure you honour that relationship by being the best you can to others.

Use Your Past to Your Advantage

We explored how to reclaim your past, and hopefully you're on the journey to doing so. Combining this with the understanding that you're an unfinished novel can bring some power and an advantage into your life. It is not often that as a marginalized community we get to say we have the upper hand, but I truly believe that we do. Not in the sense that we're better than anyone else. I don't believe in elitism. We have seen the darker corners of the world and human emotion, so now we can actively look for the light! Moving forwards you will look for the choices that bring light into your life. You will choose the path that brings you joy, and you will also extend that to other people.

The past is and always will be the past. It has no control over the future. This should always bring you joy and hope.

💜 💜 💜

Evolution and evolving as a person is so important to me. I look forward to seeing who I'll become and what I will learn. Especially being non-binary, my identity is always evolving with me and I really enjoy that. I like the fluidity of my identity. Being comfortable with self-development and personal growth is something we should all embrace.

There is nothing worse than being stuck in harmful and toxic ways that affect you and others around you. Knowing that I evolve brings me peace, because I know I will get to where I need to be, or where I want to be, eventually. This process of personal evolution keeps me positive.

Non-binary people themselves bring me hope, especially on social media. The strength of non-binary people who are putting themselves out there, opening up well overdue conversations that up until now have been discouraged by other people because they don't understand. This brings me hope for future generations of non-binary people too. It is creating more space for the community, and is making it a safer space for us too.

💜 💜 💜

Az Franco (he/him), artist and activist

No One Has It All Figured Out

To round off this chapter, I thought it would be helpful to remind you of some comforting facts.

First, no one has it all figured out! This may seem hard to believe, but no matter how successful, bold or confident a person may feel, they will always have their doubts and hang-ups. This is a true human trait, and although it can be hard to live through, it can offer you reassurance.

On my darker days, I suffer with imposter syndrome. My successes don't stand up to those of my peers. I feel very doubtful about my impact on this earth. *This is normal.* Most people suffer from this through their lives, and as the author of this book, offering you advice, I hope you can see that there is no perfect place you will arrive at.

There is so much pressure on everyone to find themselves. As non-binary people, we have doubled this pressure by asserting more control over who we are. In reality a lot of people don't ever find themselves. They are also plagued by the emotions of being people. So the fact that you are on the road to working out who you are in terms of your gender identity means you are already in a very good place.

Allow these words to relieve some pressure from the burden that you may feel, because truly no one has it all figured out. That is okay!

Key Takeaways from This Chapter

- 💜 Life is full of endless possibilities!
- 💜 Your future is not written yet, never forget that!

- ♥ No one has the right to invalidate your experience and feelings.
- ♥ We all deserve to live our days in an environment that allows us to reach our full potential.
- ♥ Limit interactions with anyone who gaslights you.
- ♥ Relationships should always be two-way streets.
- ♥ No one has it all figured out!

Chapter 5

What's Your Pleasure?

I am not sure of what your intentions were when you originally picked up this book. Perhaps skimming through the first few chapters, you may have the impression that this book is not the positive set of words you were looking for, and if you choose to read chronologically I can see how you may have come to that assumption. Let me tell you those initial words were about grounding your life and making sure you were aware of the intentions of others. From here on out the book focuses fully on you, and where better to start than with the core focus of this book: personal joy, ergo pleasure.

What Is Pleasure?

Pleasure is a word we all know and would assume to understand, but, in the context of yourself, do you know what pleasure means for you? Finding pleasure as non-binary people can be hard, purely because so many aspects of our lives have been crap. This may be due to living circumstances, family members, unsupportive friends or not living your truth.

So, when trying to bring you a series of ideas that would make your life better, pleasure was at the top of my list. Non-binary people deserve pleasure, and I say this because I don't think we hear it enough. We really do deserve it, but because of the way life is for us, we have to do a bit more legwork to find it.

Our minds are clever, but bless us, humans are easily fooled! When we were children on long car journeys, my sister and I would count certain colours of cars. Whoever saw the most won. Suddenly the hunt for yellow cars would make them seem omnipresent, but there weren't more yellow cars on the road – we were just actively looking for them! Our brains were tricked!

When we wake up in a certain mindset, that mood pursues us through our day. We are looking for it. Soon we believe that this is how our day should be! When the media whips up rubbish about the non-binary community, it can put our backs up. We enter all interactions on the back foot. This is the energy we take into our day. This means we see less pleasure in our lives.

We can't change everything in our lives. There are always good and bad parts, but if we look for more pleasure in our lives, we will find it. Carry on reading to find out how to focus your life on a pleasurable existence.

Gender Euphoria

In the community we often talk of gender dysphoria. This is a subject that could fill an entire book on its own, but essentially is a term used to explain the feelings of distress someone might feel when their gender identity does not match the body they were born in.

Gender euphoria is not the opposite of gender dysphoria, but it is often left out of the conversation. We see gender dysphoria as a red flag that someone is *only* unhappy, but it is not so simple. We can experience gender euphoria at the same time, and this is an example of the duality of being human. Gender euphoria is those moments when the light shines through the clouds of being and the wonderful effects of being yourself make life such a joy!

I cannot say when it will happen, how often it will happen or the longevity of these instances, but these are the moments that make life worth living.

Where to Look for Pleasure

So if your eyes are eagerly scanning the world for yellow cars, where would you go to see more? Well, a busy road with loads of cars is a great place to be. Life isn't so simple, sadly. To find pleasure in life, we have to work out what brings it and what doesn't.

I am not a minimalist, and probably never will be, so Marie Kondo has never been a massive part of my life. However, her method of decluttering rooms – asking if each item sparks joy – can be applied to finding pleasure. If it does not bring you joy, do not interact with it. The things that do bring you joy are the things that you should cling on to.

When written down like that it sounds super simple. Perhaps it could be if life didn't get in the way. That is to say that some days will have less pleasure: doing a big food shop, finishing a big project, doing chores or rearranging your phone's home screen! Pleasure has to be worked into and around your routine of life admin, but should be a big focus and become a routine in itself!

Pleasure Is Free

Pleasure doesn't have to cost a penny, nor does it have to be planned. You can find pleasure in some of the smallest parts of life. Read a book from cover to cover, watch a film from your childhood, clean your makeup brushes or go for a walk and discover the world immediately around you.

Pleasure is anything that takes your mind off the hard realities of life, makes you feel safe and ultimately brings you comfort combined with joy. This may just seem like distracting yourself, but pleasure is here to enrich your life and makes the darker corners fade away.

Know What Stops Pleasure

Seeking out what brings your life pleasure is key. You also have to be aware of the situations and things that suck pleasure from your life. This requires a small amount of conscious thought and is easy to reflect upon after the fact. Some situations or interactions will be overtly devoid of pleasure, but others will be harder to uncover. If a situation, meeting or task leaves you feeling uneasy or anxious, ask yourself why.

There will have been something. Ruminating on it will allow it to come to the forefront of your mind. Was it a certain person, location, conversation topic or just a recurring comment? Once you investigate bad experiences like this, you will have a list of things that guzzle pleasure from your life, allowing you to avoid them strategically and purposefully.

We cannot cut everything that we don't like from our lives, but, out of respect for ourselves, we can set boundaries. Boundaries allow you to swerve conversation topics. They give you the power to say 'I don't feel comfortable talking about this; let's talk about something else.' Boundaries let you set time limits for people who don't respect you fully, and boundaries put your needs above those of others – something that you truly deserve!

Today versus Tomorrow

Anxiety can be a very big part of our lives. When you face a backlash to your existence, this anxiety can be heightened. Certain parts of our lives can cause us less pleasure and more worry.

Earlier, we explored how our brains are very easily tricked. I will reiterate it here – when it comes to worry and pleasure, I try to split the emotional discourse that is going on in my head. I focus on what I need to worry about right now and the things that can wait until tomorrow.

This is not mind over matter, reader. This is emotional prepping! Essentially we are limiting the emotional outlay on individual events in our lives, and not pursuing unanswerable questions in advance. This places a protective fence around your wellbeing right now and makes today easier to bear. It might even allow you to bring pleasure into the equation.*

Honestly, this may not work for you, but this is okay. Some problems are too big to forget about today. Here, I would urge you to speak to someone you are very close to. You should never suffer in silence. Sharing a worry with others helps place perspective and reduces some of the pressure.

Pleasure Presets

A bad day can floor all of us. But, if we have a reserve of things that bring us pleasure, we can wipe away some of the hassle and grief.

If you are struggling to find things that immediately bring you pleasure, then look no further than this list of things that might just

---

* No maths experience required!

be the silver lining your day needed! I have also left you room to add in your own pleasure presets so that on darker days you can come back to this page and bring yourself a little personal joy!

- Listen to your favourite song at full volume.
- Write a letter – you don't have to send it.
- Binge your favourite show – you know, the one you've seen 46 times before!
- Got a dog? Grab them and go for a walk no matter the weather!
- Turn your phone off and lose yourself in your favourite book.
- Take a bath – dig out some candles to make it into a Zen spa moment.
- Are you a budding artist? Start your next masterpiece.
- Organize your living space.
- Explore the shapes in the clouds.
- Got a bike? Ride it then!
- Pop a podcast on and actually listen to it!
- If you like phone calls, call a friend.
- Have a nap – zzzzz.
- Grab your phone and take some pictures of the world around you.
- Make a time capsule.
- Have a dance while listening to an album – I love *Confessions on a Dance Floor* by Madonna!
- Are you a yoga fan? Get your downward dog on!
- Have a mindfulness moment – meditate for five minutes.
- Try learning a new skill: French perhaps, or what about origami? Bien sûr!

Add a few personal ones of your own...

- _____
- _____
- _____
- _____

How to Increase Your Pleasure Revenue

When we discuss pleasure, we often see it as an outgoing and not an income. Let me tell you, reader, this is flawed thinking! Pleasure is a good thing. It nourishes your life. This means we need to know how to bring in the enjoyment!

Can pleasure be something that helps bring more allies into your life? Sharing pastimes and pleasures with others is a great way to bolster your sense of self. It can also create a community. Online book clubs, Zoom quizzes and group chats can be great ways to increase your pleasure revenue.

Perhaps pleasure will be the thing that improves your relationship with the world around you. Learning to love your environment takes time, but will offer you solace when you need it. Whatever form pleasure takes in your life, seeing it as a positive attribute can only be a good thing.

♥   ♥   ♥

In the beginning drag was a place where I could express myself without really knowing what it was I was expressing. I knew that I felt different towards gender, my body and things like that. It was about having a safe space for myself to compartmentalize that because I didn't know how else to do that. I didn't know anyone else that felt like me, I just knew I had an innately more feminine quality to me, and I didn't understand how else to explore that. So drag was escapism for me, and that brought me pleasure.

It brings me a lot of pleasure to know that in some respect it's never going to be perfect, but the world is going to be maybe a better place, and we're going to be able to live as fully as we want to. Drag saved my life, and I don't think I would be here today if it wasn't for it. Drag taught me to fall in love with so many parts of myself.

♥   ♥   ♥

Grace Shush (they/them), drag artist

Self-Love Is Currency

Pleasure is the basic way to love your life. It can be unlocked with self-love. I feel that self-love gets overlooked for many reasons. The body-positive movement and its messages, which were created by powerful black and POC women, have been dissolved by an audience they weren't intended for. It has now absorbed self-love and can perpetuate some harmful ideas.

I don't know if you know this, but as non-binary people, we are self-love experts. I will give you a moment to take that in...

We Really Are Experts at This!

We have fought for who we are while being seen as narcissistic trend followers. We wouldn't have made all the choices and sacrifices we have made if we didn't love ourselves! The language we use internally and externally is one of the biggest ways we can show ourselves so much love. It is important not only to seek pleasure but also to allow it to strengthen the relationship that you have with yourself.

The next time you have an internal struggle or a dark day, ensure that you treat yourself with the love that you deserve and require. Be mindful of the fact that your experiences of the world so far have opened your eyes to so much pain. However, through that pain, you have persevered and are blooming into the wonderful and unique person that you are. That is true self-love. It is currency for a life filled with pleasure and positivity.

Key Takeaways from This Chapter

♥ Remember duality exists, and it means you can let more joy into your life.

♥ When you look for it, you will find more pleasure.

♥ Use boundaries to control the way other people affect you.

♥ Remember to share how you feel with close allies – a problem shared is a problem halved.

♥ Find things that make you happy and stick to them!

♥ Self-love is very important when it's done properly.

♥ Pleasure is your right, not a choice – go out and get it!

Self-Love Word Search

We can all find it hard to show ourselves the love we truly deserve. Well, spoiler alert, reader, the world isn't kind to us, so we have to be our own support systems! To help you on the way to truly loving yourself and the pleasure-focused life around you, seek out what you need in this self-love word search!

```
a m l t d o o t s r i a p e r e q h u l
b s p v i e e o v o i c e t s b e e q d
y o t e f a n n e s p a c e x c s f o r
z l q s r y z j o y b v l b e l i e f p
i a h s m m t v c z b r l z x a e c l y
h c e s f y i i z u d z o z g u v o s f
i e r s y j v s l x i n v w t g r m b z
o b u e s x f f s a o m e p r h e p q d
o f o n f q k i h i u c p r u t s a q b
w z n d r b b x s v o q b o h e e s e p
h g o n k n a u c y p n e t r r d s f h
a d h i g d l r a t d l h d c t j i n k
s n p k d c a e l i r f e e t e a o z n
t e b y n z n s m v i l q a m p p n t e
h k l i t y c c b i h e x t s i e s t w
m e g k r w e w d t d n r p y u t a e i
t n a y u t o x q i g h b y y o r u c r
g i m z s r q n r s x g s k w n w e q e
u h i j t z x p n o i t a i c e r p p a
a s s h l e u c l p w o p g l r t m x s
```

appreciation balance belief calm compassion deserve equality
honour important inclusion joy kindness laughter love peace
permission pleasure positivity pride repair respect self
shine solace space tears time trust voice worth

Chapter 6

Self-Awareness

Pleasure is not the only tool that you need to employ to enjoy your life. It would be careless to ignore some of the other pressures that can be piled on your existence.

I outlined earlier that other people are the root cause of so many of the issues we face. Knowing this is not enough to help you day to day. Self-awareness is your responsibility! Ensure you are vigilant in avoiding triggers, labour and uneven relationships.

Don't Force Your Identity

One of the things people reach out to me about is whether they are non-binary enough. I will say this time and time again – there is no one fixed way to be non-binary. That is why we are so magical. Non-binary is anything that works for you that sits outside cisgender identities and ideals.

When it comes to the way the world sees us, some of you reading this may feel your expression of gender doesn't visibly fit the way society thinks non-binary is supposed to be. Please trust me when I say this: do not force your identity. There is no tick box experience that you need to fit into, no one sexuality that you are supposed to be and no one way to look.

The very fact that you could even feel like this is because of the pressure of society and the people around you. You only ever have to please yourself. Present how you want to. When being self-aware we have to ensure that we don't force our identity. Instead, allow it to evolve over time.

We Don't Need to Defend Our Existence

As you are probably aware, a lot of the people that you meet will have no qualms about questioning every decision you make and the motives behind them. This is very much a typical encounter for us. It doesn't mean we don't feel anything at that moment.

In these interactions it almost feels like you are on trial, defending all the non-binary people in the world, and this is your only chance to speak up for our existence. As dramatic as this sounds, it really is not your responsibility. You may be that person's first encounter with a non-binary person, but that does not mean you need to have all the answers for them.

You are not a representative for all non-binary people. Life is not like Eurovision! We are all separate people, and I want you to know that! Douze points for you, chérie!

If You Focus on It, You Will Feel Pressure

Mind over matter is something that is prioritized by less empathetic people, especially when discussing mental health. This is the idea that you can overcome issues simply by saying it's not an issue anymore. This is flawed, outdated thinking. In terms of deep-rooted trauma and mental discourse, this is never the right answer.

There is, however, something we can take from this system of thinking for our benefit. By giving less space to the microaggressions in our life, we give those things less cerebral weight. They are still a real and sometimes hurtful part of being us, but it takes some of the searing sting away. Day to day, knowing that this might happen is tough, but you also know that in reality it's not a personal attack on you and the very fabric of being you, more a societal gripe.

When we constantly focus on the way we are treated by those around us, it becomes an overwhelming presence in our lives and feels like a burden. Trust me! I've been there: unable to move on from being stared at in the street, unable to cope with silence when I enter spaces with other people and deeply offended by mild comments. I am not saying I have moved above this, more that I have found giving myself more time to think about other things a better way to spend my energy.

When we focus on the negative, it begins to suck joy from the positive. The act of overworking a problem like this drains our energy, and it makes it harder for us to find joy. If we can focus less on how we are treated by the world, and more on how we would like to live our lives, we give less energy to the draining power of focusing on our treatment. We know, sadly, those irritations will always be there, but the way we treat and deal with them can change and evolve.

Subsequently, there is time left for the attainment of pleasure. Maybe, in this circumstance, adjusting the meaning of mind over matter could be a healthy way to approach this part of your life. We can take a gawping cis man, and instead of this attention feeling like a slap across the face, we know we are on the right path to disrupt the cis-tem!

Remember to Live

I want to build on what you have just read, and remind you to live, darling! This might seem like an odd reminder because the very fact that you are reading my words means that you are living – stick with me on this one! Just existing is not living. I know this to be true from my own life! When was the last day that you truly focused on yourself and took no notice of the world around you?

Spoiler alert – this is how some of the most privileged people in the world live! Seriously, the mega rich cause the most damage to this world and don't even have to think about it. Yet if I dare to pop into the Co-op in a heel, suddenly I am causing a commotion. As a marginalized community, we are seen as an oppressed group. You know the patriarchy loves that for us, but it doesn't define us. In time we are going to take over the world one way or another, but that doesn't mean we can't enjoy ourselves while we work on that!

By remembering to live our lives, and doing so fully with a pleasure-centric approach, we spend less time on the things that erase pleasure from our routines. This is just a kind reminder again, dear reader, that you should be putting yourself first! I want you to care about your pleasure unreservedly. If you want to serve a look in Tesco, then do it – be the unexpected item in everyone's bagging area, darling!

Know Your Triggers

When being self-aware, one of the things we often forget to mitigate for is external factors that affect us internally. We call these triggers. They are unique topics and subjects that we have a personal connection or past experience with. Triggers can dredge up bad memories, bring up unresolved trauma or upset us because of their effect.

Triggers are very human. We all have them. Being aware of them allows you to avoid their impact daily. This can lead to an easier, more pleasure-centric life. I have purposely avoided giving you examples here. I don't want to trigger you. There are plenty of tips and exercises you can employ to help you online.

Having an awareness of triggers is healthy. It allows you to focus on your own life energy balance. It also gives you a framework to approach new situations, weigh up how much they may cause you to feel triggered and make a risk assessment for yourself. We cannot erase the pain some things may cause us. By knowing your triggers, you can certainly reduce their impact.

The Teacher Dilemma

When I meet new people and casually bring up my pronouns, I always end up spending the first 10–15 minutes of that interaction giving a free lesson on my identity and what it means to be non-binary. Being in certain situations can cause us to feel like we have to be 'gender teachers', educating others on the ins and outs of our lives.

This is exhausting, and, to be honest, if I wanted to educate every day I would have trained to be a teacher and collected that salary, darling! It can be so frustrating, especially when there are situations where a smartphone could have answered all the questions. My grandma – that's Shirley to you – has access to the internet and could very easily type her questions and answer them for herself. If Shirley can make that effort, then people meeting you for the first time can also do that.

This message goes out to cisgender people. Please direct your overly personal questions to your chosen internet browser. Non-binary people are not educators. We're people, and we might just like to be left alone. Google doesn't have feelings, but we do, darling!

Be Open in Your Dialogue with Others

Conflict is gross. Hands up if you hate conflict too? I am sure you face plenty of conflict in your day-to-day life because certain cisgender people disagree with you just being you! When it comes to being self-aware and putting yourself first, it can feel like every time you open your mouth, you could walk on an indignant cisgender landmine. I hate that we have to feel like this. With a little bit of reading (the next couple of paragraphs) you might just feel better about this.

Prefacing in conversations is a really useful technique to employ here. Put simply, prefacing allows you to let the other person know that what you are about to say is not a criticism, nor is it an invitation to an argument. You are simply stating how you feel.

An example of this could be a conversation with a pronoun naysayer:

> *Pronoun naysayer:* 'They' is not singular; you are being grammatically incorrect.

> *You:* I really appreciate that you may have never met anyone who uses they/them pronouns before, and this may feel new or 'alien' to you. I use they/them and I deserve you to respect this, and I don't want to debate this with you any further.

Another example of this could be a conversation about a disappointing ruling in the High Court:

> *Local Twitter news anchor:* Oh, have you seen so and so lost that appeal about hormone blockers in the High Court today?

> *You:* I haven't had the chance to look at the news yet, but I find topics like that to be quite distressing. Do you think we could talk about [insert culturally relevant nugget of drama] instead?

This initial sentence plants the other person firmly in a place to listen, and at that moment you let them know you're not critiquing them or having a go. Instead, you are being open to a conversation, but unlike so many others, you are not giving away power. Hopefully you will not be drawn into a conflict-focused interaction.

Using your own feelings in this is also helpful. It reminds the other person that you are a human, which so many people forget!

The Power of Setting Boundaries

So now you are aware of how some people's misguided behaviour can affect you and be a burden upon you, what do you do now?

Quite simply, enjoy the power of setting boundaries. This is simpler to write than it is to do, but this next section should provide you with a framework that will help you in different situations. They are little sentences you can drop into a conversation to help you feel less pressure.

Boundaries for your family

Mum, I know you are only trying to understand me better, but I find defining my gender identity to you quite lengthy. I have explained the basic principles and when I feel ready, I will talk to you more about it.

Boundaries for people you know really well

Hey Alex, it would be great if we didn't talk about [insert triggering/labour-intensive conversation topic] because it makes me really anxious.

Boundaries for people you know

I really appreciate your effort, but this topic is actually quite sensitive for me. Here is a great resource [offer article, Instagram account or webpage] that could answer your questions.

Boundaries for strangers

We don't know each other, and I wouldn't dream of asking you such personal questions. Please could we talk about something else?

I am sure you could come up with your own versions of this. You could use them in the way I described in the section discussing being open in your conversations (p.89).

Some people will try saying you're shutting them down by suggesting that you are only interested in yourself. This is not a valid response. You do not owe anyone a thing. If it comes to this, then it may be time to remove yourself from the situation.

💜   💜   💜

Boundaries are, largely, on a global scale something we don't talk about. I am, however, only understanding what boundaries look like to me right this second. It is a process that is ongoing; I don't have a template or a guidebook for it. Boundaries look like alone time, because it is so powerful, and is something I have not had in a long time. Having the space to do that centres me, and is a huge boundary. I'm also spending time working out what is non-negotiable for me. As trans people, we're allowed to have things we won't accept.

Knowing boundaries are fluid and that they're also not binary is a truth that can be held at the same time! Getting offline is super important too. People give time to have a bubble bath, for example, but will still be chilling there on their phone. You are still doing habitual things, which is stopping you creating the boundaries that you fully need. You're still too concerned with what other people think of you, or how many likes, comments or followers you're getting. It is so distracting. It's not about the quantity of likes, but about your quality of life.

Boundaries can make people feel like we're rejecting them, but that is on them. Rejection is redirection, is what I always say. Every time we move a boundary or create a new one, you just have to get to know us differently. That doesn't mean you can't still get to know us, there are just different ways, but a lot of people aren't that creative when it comes to finding these ways!

💜   💜   💜

Lexi Chandra (she/they), writer and model

Be Aware of the Draining Power of Labour

Being forced into becoming an educator isn't limited to strangers and new people we meet. Friendship groups can also offer potential pockets of labour. Even though these people support you, they will confuse their labour-laden behaviour with being helpful.

You might know exactly what I mean. You can sail through this, then! Some of you might find it harder to spot what labour can look like in friendship groups. To help, I have shared some examples below. I am sure you will have experienced at least one of them at some point.

Asking you to explain your gender identity fully for them again so they understand *is labour*.

Asking you to help them work out how to talk to a non-binary person at work *is labour*.

Asking you if you think x, y, z person in their life could be non-binary *is labour*.

Asking you if certain celebrities are or could be non-binary *is labour*.

Asking you to explain something that was discussed in a recent episode of *Drag Race is labour*.

All relationships have the potential for toxic behaviour. It is not the sexy kind of Toxic Ms B. Spears sold us on her futuristic jet. Sadly, we quite often get burdened with this kind of behaviour. In these situations, if they are true friends they should be very open to hearing your boundaries and, by engaging prefacing in your dialogue, you should be able to nip it in the bud. If they aren't open to this conversation and turn this back on you, then perhaps you should limit your time with this person. We don't need to throw them away, just pop them in the recycling bin. Allow them to think on their behaviour. Perhaps get them to buy a copy of this book, and see if they are up to changing for the better and, instead of draining you, stepping up their behaviour. Unless you are being paid, darling, no one is entitled to *your labour!*

Allow Yourself to Be Surprised

I would just like to say that you shouldn't go into all situations and scenarios expecting that people will treat you in a certain way. There is a chance that some people won't be hostile towards you but instead will show you respect. I thought it would be inconsiderate to everyone to paint such a bleak picture.

I am always surprised when strangers are genuinely nice to me. It does happen! Nice people are everywhere, it just feels like a massive game of 'Where's Wally', but they are worth looking for! Once you find them, your faith in humanity is restored – a little bit.

Key Takeaways from This Chapter

- 💜 Don't force your identity – you know who you are!
- 💜 You're not a representative for all non-binary people.
- 💜 Trying to give less power to microaggressions softens their impact.
- 💜 You're not a teacher – it is not your job to educate about the community.
- 💜 Boundaries can help you deal with sensitive conversation topics.
- 💜 Be aware of toxic friendships that force labour onto you!
- 💜 Not everyone you meet will be a negative force – people can still surprise you!

Self-Awareness Crossword

Being self-aware can feel like a full-time job, but it doesn't have to be a big expenditure of effort. My words are here as a guide and are not a cure-all fix. Take what you want from these words, and try techniques in your life to see if they help you.

To help consolidate some of the advice I've shared with you, have a go at my self-awareness crossword.

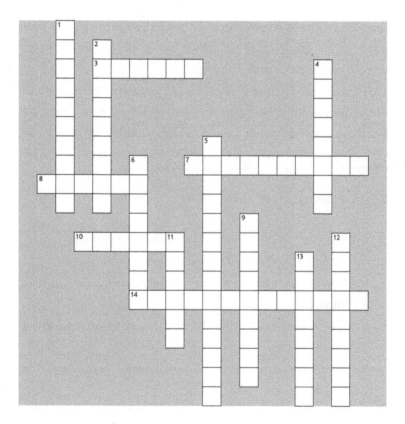

Across

3. You don't need to do this for your existence (6)

7. Methods to protect your energy (10)

8. Energy given to others (6)

10. Another way to answer a personal question (6)

14. Making sure you are considering all your needs (4,9)

Down

1. You only represent yourself (10)

2. What some cisgender people expect from you (8)

4. The way you present yourself to the world (8)

5. A friend constantly treating you as a teacher (5,9)

6. Things that can upset you (8)

9. A way to create open dialogue (9)

12. The outside focus that can affect you (9)

11. Your identity can grow with you (6)

13. When others disagree with you and want to argue (8)

Chapter 7

You Are Privileged

There are so many forks in the road that makes up our life, and for non-binary people this feels like a journey that is dictated by others. All those forks can leave you feeling that you are on someone else's route. There is no map, darling!

We forget how much privilege there is in being exactly who we are. I want to share that with you in this chapter.

What Is Privilege in the Context of Non-Binary Identities?

It might feel a little left-field that I am opening a section of this book by telling you that you are privileged, but please hear me out! Privilege is the idea that we possess something that others don't. We have become fearful of the term privilege because, in many aspects of our society, it is something we have to work through to make the world fair. An example of this is white privilege.

However, the privilege you hold as a non-binary person is not an unfair advantage over others. Actually, it is a reward that you deserve. Many of you will have been through a lot to own your identities. That struggle is worthless if there is not a pot of gold at the end of the rainbow. However, at the end of your rainbow, there *is* a pot of gold. That is the concept of privilege. You have come so far, and every day should be a celebration for you. It takes a lot to become who you truly are, and that is a gift we can all be thankful for.

It may not feel like it every day, but the clarity that comes from figuring out in some way who you are is a small gift from the universe. You cracked the code and survived. Now you get to thrive, my darling!

We're Not a Burden

I want to take this opportunity to remind you that you are not a burden. Your existence is not an issue. The world around you has tricked you into thinking this way because they are not ready to fully accept such a joyful existence. It is hard to counter this kind of thinking. While there is not much in the world that makes us feel safe, or even valid, we have to put ourselves first because the world around us does not.

The discourse we face can be tough and has given us the narrative that we are the problem in the equation. If the tables were turned, and X no longer equalled Y and cis-gender people faced three per cent of the crap we do, there would be help left, right and centre. Y does equal cisgender people always putting themselves first. We have been victimized without being offered any of the rights afforded to victims. Victims are not burdens, they have the right to be listened to and demand better treatment moving forwards. You have the right never to feel like a burden because *you are not a burden*.

The issues we face – pronoun problems, misgendering and bluster about trends – are all hurdles. You can jump over them! So not only do you know you are not a burden, but you also have the strength to overcome these issues, which is marvellous – something, I hope, that gives you hope!

You've Made It This Far

I adore simple facts. They are surprising. They can make things feel so much better. A simple fact I can deduce about you, by assumed calculations, namely that you are reading this book, is that you have made it this far as a human. In itself this seems like a small thing, but even the smallest things can make the biggest differences in our lives.

Every day you open your eyes is another day you have made it. That is something you should celebrate. That's it, you've made it this far, and you can keep on going with that knowledge. You did that! Well done to you! Simple, small, but oh so sensational, darling!

Embrace Good and Bad Days

Some days it feels like I have everything nailed down. I feel content in my sense of self, and I am working steadily on projects. That's a great day! Other days I don't always know which way is up, and I get lost in indecision. This is natural, and I have learnt to absorb this into the knowledge of what it means to be me.

Life has this habit of throwing you curve balls. It doesn't invalidate the progress you have made, and don't let these bad days make you lose sight of who you are! There will be highs, lows and countless levels in between in your future. You need to know that is to be expected.

Knowing Who You Are Is a Joyous Thing

The process of familiarizing yourself with your gender identity is not something that happened overnight, nor is it a binary yes/no process. I have spent years evolving into the person I am today, and I don't think that this is my final form. Moreover, I am on a continual path.

Yet, I will say this to you: being able to say you know in some way who you are is a joyous thing. The very fact you have gone against predetermined markers of gender and stepped outside binary gender is a massive achievement.

I don't know if you have seen the Disney film *WALL-E*, but there is a nice example I can borrow to explain this principle. When WALL-E is searching for Eve on the starliner Axiom, he inadvertently bumps into passengers Mary and John. They have become so engrossed in their automated life they are unaware of their surroundings. By knocking them out of their automated chairs, WALL-E opens their eyes to the beauty in front of them, and they suddenly begin to live their lives. There is more purpose, more reason, and life seems to bloom in the mind of the emancipated.

I would argue that being non-binary is to live life outside of the predetermined expectations. We see the true beauty of being gender diverse. It opens up all the wonders of the world to us. That is not to say that all cisgender people are living automated lives – more that they go with the flow – so how could they see the beauty of breaking away from the traditional expectations placed on them?

We as non-binary people have been thrown from our automated chairs, and life is there for us to really see for the first time. Embrace that joy, darling!

Many Cisgender People Don't Know Who They Are

I explained that cisgender people go with the flow when it comes to gender expression and the way their gender informs their life choices. I feel this is bold and will spark many cis people to send me very angry messages, but this is my book and you need to hear this, so sod 'em! If you are cisgender and offended by anything I have said, please don't hesitate to email someone who has time to waste, and that is not me!

Binary gender is meted out at birth, solely based on visible physical attributes. Genitals are the only method of determining gender, which is an incredibly arbitrary system when you think of the complex nature of humans. This bizarre system then goes on to set out rules and systems placed on that person for their entire life.

This brings me onto a very neat little nugget of information that shines a light on the hostility we face as non-binary people. Many cisgender people don't know who they are. They have never faced an identity crisis in their own body related to their own assertion of gender. They haven't had to fight to feel free in their gender identity. Suddenly seeing non-binary people using compassionate reasoning to determine their own identity could make a cisgender person nervous, because they have never felt such a strong sense of self, and they suddenly feel very threatened!

This is a generalization and is not the only device at work, but it does explain some of the hostility we have faced in our past. It is yet another example of others' problems becoming our problem to bear. Ignore that messy behaviour, and instead feel smug that you truly know who you are. You have more sense of self than most people, and that's a joyous thing!

It's Time to Celebrate Your Heightened Sense of Self

I hope by now you can begin to see how you might be in a privileged position. You have a heightened sense of self that has been honed through traumas, other people's problems and your ambition to be your true self. Some CEOs of massive companies don't do that much work in their whole careers. They have no qualms about spending millions on multiple homes, yachts and tax-avoidance schemes, so the very least we can do is celebrate who we are.

I'm not saying you need to throw yourself a party every day, but there should be some consideration for your own pleasure and the ability to derive pleasure from your existence. Enjoy the moments where the intersection of your gender identity meets your hobbies, passions and skills. The more you seek this out the more valid you will feel. Soul food in itself! Be proud of your resilience. You have been your biggest advocate. Embrace that being who you are is not the reason you live, but one of the driving forces to make your life better.

♥   ♥   ♥

Finding myself has changed everything – it has had a massive impact. It has changed the way I communicate with people, the way I check in with myself and the frequency that I check in with myself. For a long time, being an outsider from a queer perspective, we do a lot of things that aim to ingratiate ourselves with the most dominant force societally, or in the room we're in. We act a certain way, that's maybe 5–15 per cent of us, the rest of it is filtered through different perceptions and misconceptions.

Going on this journey of self-actualization – as I like to call it – I have arrived at a place where I don't feel bad for being me! It has been incredibly important to me to reach that point where I am comfortable, and okay with who I am and what I do!

It is really empowering embracing anything, everything, all of the unknowns, all of the things that I didn't know that I would be able to do. When I step back and look at myself embracing all of the possibilities that I could have been, and all of the possibilities that I still could be, stepping into that empowers those around me too. I could not be more grateful for that!

♥   ♥   ♥

Darkwah Kyei-Darkwah (they/them), artist and model

How to Ensure This Relationship Stays Strong

Now you have unlocked the magic power of your privilege, I want you to keep that feeling burning inside of you. If things get tough, or other people try to dim your shine, you have a set of actions to ensure that your light keeps on burning!

- Keep a list of all the things that you love about being non-binary. Look at it on darker days to remind yourself of your strength.
- What makes you feel confident? A favourite outfit, a certain pair of shoes or maybe makeup? Find that thing, and know you can use it when you want to bring a boost of personal confidence to your day. My secret weapon is black eyeliner. It makes me feel so powerful!
- Find role models who help you see the power of being exactly who you are. This small dose of visibility will reconnect you to yourself. For a head start look at p.198.
- Avoid being drained by rubbish media outlets. Mute certain words across social media, so that 'hot takes' don't derail a day.
- Surround yourself with IRL and digital friends who have similar interests to you so that your identity isn't the only thing that you talk about – it is healthy to create space for all of yourself.
- Embrace the diverse nature of our community and absorb other experiences. Look at other queer books and queer characters on TV and enjoy being surrounded by like-minded representation.

- Walk away from difficult people – you don't have to justify your existence or define yourself. Show them their actions are toxic by removing yourself from that situation.

Add in a few of your own:

- _____
- _____
- _____
- _____

It's a Privilege to Help Others See Their Worth

Now that you have accessed and understood your own privilege, you are in a unique position to use this newfound privilege to help other non-binary people. The best bit is that it hardly takes any time at all! Being visible in society is one of the most basic, but powerful tools to validate other people's feelings. Can you remember the first gender diverse person you saw? I remember when I left home to go to university. This was the first time I saw queer people not only existing but thriving! This was the small push I needed to explore who I was.

By being your true self, you will help other people on their journey to being their true selves. It is a very powerful and precious part of being non-binary. This small act of self-acceptance creates a chain reaction – other people who see the worth of being themselves. Think of us as non-binary dominoes!

Key Takeaways from This Chapter

- ♥ It is a privilege to know who you are!
- ♥ You are not a burden, darling.
- ♥ You have come a long way; use that as a comfort.
- ♥ Remember to celebrate who you are.
- ♥ Find ways to nourish the relationship you have with yourself.
- ♥ You can use your privilege to help other non-binary people see their worth too.
- ♥ You've done the work; enjoy your life a bit more, darling.

Celebrate Your Privilege Bingo

This chapter is here to help you see how wonderful it is to be you and why you should embrace this as power to help you move forwards with your life.

To chart your progress and celebrate being truly yourself, use this fun bingo sheet. Start your journey to celebrate your heightened sense of self. All you need to do is cross off the squares as you understand and experience them in your life! The first with a full house (all boxes crossed) wins. Dabbers at the ready, darling...

Celebrate your privilege BINGO

You know that you are not and never will be a burden!	You've watched the film WALL-E and understand the value of truly seeing your surroundings!	You've worked harder than many CEOs, so celebrating yourself is a just reward!
It is a privilege to know exactly who you are, and you should celebrate that!	*Celebrate your privilege*	You have ways to ensure your light is never dimmed by others or by bad days!
You have the right never to feel like a burden, because you are not a burden.	Every new day is a reminder that you are here, queer and WONDERFUL!	You know that by being your true self, you'll help other people on their journey too!

Chapter 8

Let's Talk About Fashion

F ashion and the art of dressing are often seen as frivolous pursuits, but the way we dress is essential to our sense of self and our ability to express our identity. Saying this is one thing, but it is not as simple as that. We don't wake up one day and have our identity magically fixed because of our wardrobe.

There are many hurdles when it comes to the way you dress and express yourself. I want to lend my years of experience and expertise when it comes to the way sartorial choices intersect with your identity.

The Fabric Reality of Clothes

One of the biggest things that I get asked all the time is how I shop for clothes as a non-binary person. It is tricky to navigate the binary world of mainstream fashion. I always have the same answer, and it is the one I will give you too – clothes are literally just pieces of fabric.

There is nothing to stop anyone in the world wearing a dress, wearing a suit or even wearing lederhosen – it's not for me, but I'm sure you'd look amazing. Clothes are inanimate fabric with no meaning imbued in them. The meaning is placed on them by society. We all know how we feel about society telling us what to do!

There is no boundary to what you can and can't wear. If it fits you, you feel comfortable and the act of wearing it brings you pleasure, then go for it! As with many of the issues we face as a community, the issues lie with other people's feelings – not your own. There are no rules. Wear whatever you want as long as it makes you happy.

Dress for *You*

We explored the idea of different levels of selfishness earlier in the book and how as non-binary people we deserve to be 'selfish'. Dressing for self-pleasure is often seen as selfish by the main-stream media and also by cis men typically called Kevin, Keith and Martin.

What people fail to understand is that dressing for pleasure is not vain. It is not a form of self-obsession. It is a compassionate act. Life is simple really and is just a set of processes that take us from cradle to grave. That might seem a bit bleak, but this is why we have the chattels of human life.

It is the things that we surround ourselves with that make being human so wonderful. Some people collect thimbles, clocks or even commemorative beer mats, so why is collecting clothes that make you happy any stranger? If anything, it is far more rational to have a wardrobe full of pleasure than it is to have 3754 beer mats, but this is a judgement-free zone, so if you like the beer mats, then run with it, darling.

Jokes aside, dressing for yourself is a truly wonderful approach to have and will unlock so much joy in your life. Give it a go!

Lack of Visibility Does Not Mean Lack of Validity

Growing up, I had no one to look up to. I knew no gender diverse people, and non-binary was not being discussed. This was one of the reasons I think it took me so long to truly discover who I was. The first time I saw another queer person was the first time I thought I could truly be who I knew I was.

I wasted years of my life ignoring the feelings inside of me. I thought they weren't valid. Lack of visibility is one of the reasons I felt lost. I cannot bear that you might feel like this too! Just because you might not have seen anyone that looks or acts like you do doesn't mean the way you feel, look and act isn't valid.

In this instance, you have to be the visibility you need in this world. Use this opportunity to put your stamp on the world by exploring who you are. Gently answer those feelings that you've perhaps been ignoring. The smallest changes can make the biggest differences. This is how I came to be me. It is a gradual process. It can be done day by day. You are in control of this process. If you never start, you will never know how it could make you feel!

The Confidence Myth

'Confidence' is one of those early 2000s buzz words that were rife on truly crap reality makeover shows. National treasure Gok Wan made a living dressing people while shouting that it is all about the confidence over a dizzy montage of happy, smiley people.

In this context, often falsely, confidence is sold as a commodity. Singular people have to own it in order to feel wonderful. Those who are not confident do not have *it*. No surprises here, reader, I am going to change the way you think about confidence!

Confidence is not about you. You do not need to have ownership of confidence. I learnt this by gracing the front row of countless London Fashion Week shows, as the largest and often only non-binary person in the room. Confidence is about mastering your emotional budget towards others.

The issue with confidence is *not you*. It's *other people's* perception of you that *is* the issue. The way we dress informs other people how to judge us, accessing the stereotypes they assume about us, because of what we picked from our wardrobe that morning. How much power you want to give this affects how great you feel. The more you focus on what makes you happy, the less other people can diminish your star quality, baby!

The Spotlight Effect

There is also another factor you need to consider to understand what confidence really means when it comes to the way you dress, and that is just how wrapped up people are. It can feel like everyone you meet might have something to say about the way you have chosen to express yourself visually. This can make you feel a bit crap! Do not despair, my darling. No one really cares that much!

One of the most exciting examples of human behaviour that I came across recently (via TikTok no less) is the spotlight effect. If you can, picture a spotlight on a stage lighting up one person. This is the visual representation of how much other people see of the world. In essence, humans are only bothered about themselves and the reach of their own influence.

It can feel as non-binary people that we are the ones in the spotlight, but truly, it is everyone else who is under their own spotlight. When you see it in this way – and trust me this *is* a reality – suddenly, the way you dress is for you and only you. It becomes a true pleasure. No one can make you feel anything other than joy in the way you dress. This is the true meaning and application of confidence, dear reader.

The Power of Glamour

Glamour is a wonderful word. It means different things to lots of people. A typical dictionary would say that glamour is 'the special, exciting and attractive quality of a person, place or activity'. Glamour is a personal context that each of us places on objects, people and places.

In the context of you right now, glamour is the culmination of dressing and the visual representation of your identity. The way that makes you feel! What is so wonderful about glamour is it makes us feel so wonderful. It sends lovely, happy-making endorphins around our bodies. It is unique to each and every one of us. I want you to see that dressing for pleasure is such a gift. How wonderful it is! Glamour is often reserved for special occasions, but *you* are a special occasion. I want you to delve deep into the power of glamour.

I feel the most glamorous in a certain dress, which was something silly like £9 years ago. It's floral with big silver sequin cuffs and hem. There is nothing that special about it, other than it sheds sequins everywhere I go, but this dress makes me feel the most glamorous version of me. Slick on some red lipstick and throw on a pair of heels I can't walk in, and I feel totally unstoppable.

Work out what makes you feel glamorous, and run with it. It will make your life even better, and on days where you feel flatter than the lips of a drag queen before *Drag Race*, you can use this ultimate glamorous look to give you all the energy you need. That is why glamour is so powerful!

Dressing is Political

As queer people, even breathing seems to catch the attention of someone. So the way we dress is surely going to say something about our stance on the world. In fact, the way we dress is truly political. By being our true selves we stand for a life that is not pre-determined by archaic boundaries placed on us by the patriarchy and its hegemonic demands.

It might not feel very drastic to you, but the way you dress says more about you than you ever could in seconds. We are then of course judged and parcelled up by onlookers' stereotyping minds, but we still have an impact.

In that moment, being truly yourself is a wonderful act of visibility. To show you how impactful that can be, imagine if you saw someone who looked like you do now when you were younger! How much of a difference would that have made for you then? It might have answered some of the questions you had about your identity. It might have kick-started your process of self-discovery earlier. It might just have reminded you that you were not alone in this world.

However you look at it, simply dressing how you want can make a big difference. So canvas your corner of the world. Make a statement every time you step out of the door.

De-gender Your Wardrobe

Quite often, even as non-binary people, we place gendered expectations on the things in our lives. This concerns our wardrobes. I want to give you a list of tips that have helped me explore my style and allowed me to feel more comfortable wearing everything my heart desires.

- Always remember that comfort is key – the first question to ask yourself is 'Do I feel comfortable?' Physical comfort goes a long way to help provide mental comfort.

- If something feels very new and almost scary, break it in at home first. I don't know if you wore your new school shoes the last week of the summer holidays, but I always did, so that the first day back wouldn't be hampered by blisters and pinched toes. Employ this tactic for new and exciting items. It will take the shock away when you go out in them for the first time.

- Pair bold new items with familiar favourites. The first time I wore dresses, I would always layer them with jeans, because the familiarity of jeans made the dress feel far less daring. Just like long tops! So bring familiarity to new and bold items in your wardrobe!

- When looking to branch out sartorially, keep some elements similar to your current wardrobe. Pick colours, textures and patterns that you already wear a lot. This will make the garment feel more comfortable.

- Don't be scared of risks. Embrace them. Risks are always phrased as scary, but without risks how will you know if they will pay off? It is far riskier to live a life without risks!

- *Do not ask contentious people for their opinion.* You already know they will tell you they think what you're wearing is a disaster, so don't go there!

- Take photos of your outfits. Get used to seeing yourself in a way that fully represents your identity. The more at ease you are with the way you look, the less nerve racking it will be!

- *Do not ask contentious people for their opinion!* Seriously, don't!

♥ ♥ ♥

Letting go of the expectation to dress in a particular way helped me to understand my style and the way I want to present my-self to the world, and what gender expression means to me as a non-binary person. Growing up I wasn't expected to dress in a particular way in terms of my family, they always gave me the space to wear whatever I wanted. Yet I did feel the pressure to look feminine and have long hair because I am AFAB [assigned female at birth]. I felt that from outer influences coming in, it wasn't something that was sparking from the inside.

I went through so many years of having that compulsory femininity placed on me, to then reject all of that, and dressing in a way that was very masc. It wasn't how I was completely feeling, or completely how I wanted to dress. I was rejecting everything that was imposed on me, and now I'm in a place where I am embracing what I like because I like it, the aesthet-ics and how I feel.

If I could give any advice, it is not to let others dictate the way you dress and the way you present. It is your own sense of self, and it is valid. This is what I wanted to hear when I was in that process of understanding how I wanted to dress and how I saw myself despite all the expectations and objections because of my gender.

♥ ♥ ♥

Jordan Benedetti (they/them), activist and speaker

Weaponize Your Wardrobe

This might come as a shock to you, but dressing for pleasure can help you deal with other people. In short, the way you choose to dress and present yourself can begin to form an armour that you can either find comfort and solace in, or use for power and to diffuse tension caused by other people.

Dressing is fun. It can also be an ally to you in tricky situations. The choices you make in front of the mirror can be a power source that you can lean into and provide you with energy that radiates your true self and emphasizes your place in the world.

I find when I feel my best self, and have tapped into the power of glamour, people who want to derail my happiness have a much harder time finding their target. My visual identity is part of me, I am part of it, and that weaponizes my wardrobe for the trickier days in my existence. It can do the same for you too!

Non-Binary Friendly Brands

I get asked about my wardrobe *all* the time, so I thought I would share some of the brands I have loved and worked with that make me feel like the icon I am.

Universal brands I love:

- Lucy & Yak – dungarees are a must, kids!
- Collusion at ASOS.
- Lazy Oaf – wild knitwear and more.
- Loud Bodies – the most romantic dresses you'll ever see, plus they go up to 10XL – we love to see it!
- Kina and Tam (not fully size inclusive) – for cosy separates and cardigans.

- Telfar – very pricey and collections sell out in minutes, but a lovely brand all the same!

Gendered brands, but still great clothes:

- Marks and Spencer – wild, but they do the best trousers and coats!
- Vivienne Westwood – some amazing shoes – very pricey, but totally worth saving up for.
- Shrimps – for the teeny-tiny bags of your dreams – very pricey, but who doesn't deserve nice things?
- Seasalt – amazing striped T-shirts and separates, with great ethics and sizing.

Key Takeaways from This Chapter

- ♥ Clothes are literally just pieces of fabric!
- ♥ Dressing for you is a compassionate act.
- ♥ Just because you might not have seen anyone who looks or acts like you do doesn't mean the way you feel, look and act isn't valid.
- ♥ Confidence is not about you. The more you focus on what makes you happy, the less other people can diminish your star quality, baby!
- ♥ Work out what makes you feel glamorous, and run with it.
- ♥ Being truly yourself is a wonderful act of visibility.
- ♥ Dressing for yourself can bring you so much power. Lean into that!

Chapter 9

Self-Expression

The media is slowly opening its arms to the idea of diversity and showing inclusivity to the transgender community. As a result, non-binary visibility and awareness are on the increase. However, this is causing some slight optical issues, as certain people are becoming the face of our community.

The glorious nature of being outside the binary is lost on the masses, and this is creating a concept of conformity. This section is here to remind you that there is no right way to *look* or *be* non-binary.

'Every Expert Was Once a Beginner'

Now I know how unhelpful well-known sayings can be. They are often used in a way (usually by mums on Facebook) that makes it seem as if they are super obvious and that we're all silly for not knowing them. Well, Maureen, misquoting a dead, white, cisgender man isn't that helpful to me!

So let's return to 'every expert was once a beginner'. Knowing that all experts had to start somewhere is comforting, and so I will happily give those six words a little bit of space in these pages. Quite simply, I am using these words to tell you that we all have to start somewhere. No matter how shaky the first steps are, they will always lead to more confident steps in the future. Without those shaky steps, there is no future! When it comes to expressing your gender identity, take it at your own pace. Don't be rushed. You will know what feels right, but you have to start somewhere!

If you're interested, the quote is attributed to legendary actress Helen Hayes (no, I haven't seen any of her films either!), who in her career won an Emmy, a Grammy, an Oscar and a Tony – only 1 of 16 who have achieved this – so her advice seems to be very pertinent in terms of starting from the bottom and working your way up to becoming an icon. Cheers to you, Ms Hayes!

The Hoops

One of the first forays I had into visually distancing myself from binary gender was through earrings. It is a very small thing but at the time felt very groundbreaking to me. I chose to buy a pair of U-shaped silver hoops that dropped three centimetres from my ears.

I still have them, and today they are something I would choose for a dressed-down look, but at the time they felt so feminine to me. The boldness of my choice sent electricity through my body, and it felt so huge not only to have the thought to try something different but to give that thought approbation.

That positive experience would be the one I would use to justify other perceived risks in the future. I would say the hoops were my very first shaky steps on my journey to visually expressing myself fully. So this is your reminder to give yourself permission, darling. It will all work out great!

The Only Way to Know If Something Is Right Is to Try It

I am a fussy eater and have always been like this. When I was younger, my mum would never force me to eat things I didn't like, but she would ask me to try them for her. Obviously it meant in the long run that she was right, I would end up liking what she had put so much effort into, but also it meant that I didn't miss out on the majesty of shepherd's pie.

Negotiation in this sense is something that I have applied to other questions that arise in my head, usually pertaining to my visual identity. I never knew what it would feel like to wear heels until I did it, but had I not tried, I wouldn't know. The risk associated with the hoops is far less than the perceived risk the first time I wore heels, but had I not tried the hoops, I would never have had the courage to try heels. Now I feel so at home in six-inch platforms that I can't imagine a life without them.

Thanks for all the effort and love, Mum, you taught me such a good life lesson. We should all try things at least once. We will find the things that we love, and you were right, shepherd's pie is truly wonderful!

Self-Doubt Is Normal – How to Ignore It

Throughout this book I have attributed so many of the issues that we face as a community to others around you. However, this one is something that we all do to ourselves. Self-doubt! It is normal. It is expected when trying new things for the first time.

Intrusive thoughts are something that you should know about. These are unwelcome thoughts that can distress us. Doubt is a very mild form of intrusive thoughts. It is something you should watch out for, because over time, left unchecked, doubt can alter the relationship you have with yourself.

Doubt can be dealt with in a very similar way to the way that we dealt with our inner saboteur. Acknowledge it, and then choose to honour a different approach by using the positive affirmation of how wonderful certain actions can make you feel. This can be seen as a technique of reasoning with yourself. Remember how great you felt when you did x, y, z? Apply that to the next thing you want to try!

Continuous application of this method, and the more risks you take, will make doubt so much easier to overcome. It will turn up less frequently to try to derail your progress.

💜 💜 💜

On paper, it makes sense that not every avenue in life may work out for us, and eventually we need to find our own spaces. At the same time, I know that all those forays are necessary to figure out what works for me. I still would like the opportunity to do those things even if they don't work. At the end of the day, it will guide me to something that will. And honestly, there also needs to be room for avenues to change because we may not necessarily stick with one.

Initially, I saw dance as the way to express my non-binary identity. As I have delved deeper, I have realized that fashion can do that also — so dressing up helps me too. Filmmaking is helping me as well. There are all these different mediums, and there shouldn't need to be one definitive thing because we are not one definitive thing. Not just as non-binary people, but all people, we constantly evolve.

When people say to me that I am living my most authentic self, I always think that the person who I am after that interaction will not be the same. The person who I will be tomorrow is not the same person that I am today; I am constantly evolving, changing, adapting and growing. Making peace with that is very helpful for me because in knowing that I don't need to stick to one form of self-expression, I can have that multidisciplinary aspect to myself. The essence of being non-binary is the rejection of anything rigid, allowing yourself to be in the moment and feeling what is right for you!

💜 💜 💜

Shiva Raichandani (he/they), performance artist

Don't Solicit Opinions from
Those Who Don't Support You Fully

One way to decrease the power that doubt can have over you is to block out the opinions of naysayers. I spoke about not soliciting opinions from other people earlier in the book. I would like to expand upon this. Opinions are wonderful, because we all have them, and they show the variation of the human experience, which is marvellous. However, some people confuse their own opinion with the *only* way someone or something can be. This is why other people's opinions can derail your own progress.

Obviously the types of people who think like that are the ones who offer their opinions for free. We cannot stop that, but we can ensure that we aren't subjected to their toxic thoughts when we don't need them! It is nice to be buoyed up by supporting advice, but unhelpful negative opinions are not what you need to hear when you are trying something for the very first time.

In this kind of situation, I would either not engage in conversation, or, if conversation is unavoidable, change the subject. I used to be a nail technician, and keeping a conversation flowing with clients is key to making them like you and tip, but this can be tricky. I found that the weather was always a passive and comfortable topic to talk about, and I spent many a manicure talking about rain!

So, if you are trying a new look, and someone tries to crash into your great day with their truckload of self-righteous opinions, just ensure you mention how bad/good/wet/cold/dry/hot the weather has been, and halt that negative conversation before it even starts, darling.

Take Your Self-Development at Your Own Speed

If you know any non-binary angels, or perhaps follow them on Instagram – *cough, @benpechey cough, follow me* – then you will witness other people's magical metamorphosis, or you will come in on their sixth year of self-exploration. I urge you not to feel pressure from other people's beauty.

We are all on separate paths. Although these paths can converge, you are a unique human being. Your timeline is just for you. There is no rush to do anything. I want you to know that you can take all the time in the word, or go as quickly as you want to. You shouldn't make that decision based on anyone else, anywhere.

I am sure that I am not finished working out who Ben is. I am really happy in who I am right now, but there is no finished destination that plonks me in a neat, specific box. The goal has always been freedom from binary ideals placed on me. So, I have no expectations or strict ideas of my trajectory, more that I want to continue to honour what brings me joy and seek out happiness by expressing exactly who I am in the moment.

This is something I urge you to pay close attention to. It is key in being self-aware, my darlings. Make sure that you work at your own speed. Take your self-development one day at a time in the best way that makes you happy!

How to Navigate Comments Like 'You're So Brave'

If you asked me to compile a list of things that sound like an insult, but are supposed to be a compliment, then 'You're so brave' would come straight in at number one. I understand the sentiment behind comments like this, because the other person in the interaction feels like they are being nice. However, take it from me, this is not a compliment, Cheryl!

When hapless cases like Cheryl say that to you, it signals that the way you present is very extreme to them – bless their fragile view of the world – hence the bravery! Yet, for you, it's just another casual Wednesday afternoon. This is a prime example of our community being singled out.

These comments are super frustrating and, when they catch you off guard, can be derailing. As with so many of the concepts covered in these pages, I cannot stop this happening, but I can give you a thought process to remedy a situation like the one Cheryl has put us in.

It isn't bravery that Cheryl is witnessing. It's the realization that she has never been able to pinpoint exactly who she is visually. You are not brave, but Cheryl's approach to life seems less exciting. So, to cover her cowardice, she must 'other' your experience. When cishet people try to compliment us in this manner, they simply enhance their own mediocrity! You can take this comment in your stride and turn it on its head. Cheryl basically told us that she is 'oh so bland', and isn't that sad?!

The Power of Makeup

Makeup is magic! My mind cannot be changed on that fact. I have no idea why recent history has made makeup a femme-presenting-person-only item. Everyone can enjoy makeup. Who wouldn't want to make their face look the best it can and play with colours and textures?

The day I began to explore makeup was a truly great one. I think I started with eyebrows at a press event years ago. Then, over the next 18 months, I began to explore different parts of my face and where makeup worked for me, what I could change and where I could enhance. If you are thinking of getting into makeup then I would like to share some tips with you.

- Remember the words of Helen Hayes, 'every expert was once a beginner'. My first attempts at winged liner were, thankfully, not documented. They were incredibly shaky, and looked like plans for a rollercoaster! Expect the first time to be the worst. Build on that! Before you know it, your winged liner will be sharp enough to cut through the crap we face in society!

- Start slowly – no one can do everything all at once. Gradually trying things will help you learn as you go along. Watch other people apply makeup – this is the *best* way to learn. Dutch trans icon Nikkie de Jager – a.k.a. NikkieTutorials – has taught me pretty much everything I know over the years.
- Start cheap – expensive products work just the same as more budget-friendly ones when you are new at makeup, so start with budget brands and build up to pricey items when you're more experienced. Once you have mastered certain skills, invest in good products to help you hone that skill – black eyeliner and red lipstick is my signature and I spend good money on my cult items. They give the biggest boosts.
- Trial and error is the best way to approach it. Not everything will work. Some things will be a happy accident! You will only find that out through experimentation, darling!
- You are still you with makeup on, and vice versa. This is not about changing who you are, but more about refining and honing how you want to present to the world. Use that energy to own the day.

Makeup Brands I Love

If you are considering entering the glamorous world of putting cosmetics on your face, then there are some brands you need to know about!

- DEPIXYM: This brand has one of the most open approaches to makeup. Creating products based on functionality and multiple use, DEPIXYM is deliciously devoid of binary

THE BOOK OF NON-BINARY JOY

exceptions. Known for its cosmetic emulsions that can be used everywhere, cruelty free and *vegan*. I am a repeat purchaser of shade #0371, and my eyebrows never look anything less than perfect! They are the multiuser, multiuse products worth investing in, darling!

- Jecca Blac: Jecca Blac offers a brand that is open to all beauty lovers with a product line that represents all expressions and intersections of gender identities and sexuality. With resources for transgender people, education and transformative products, which are also cruelty free. I am a massive fan of the glow drops, which make my skin radiant!

- Too Faced: This brand does nothing revolutionary for our community. However, its jet black liquid eyeliner 'Better than Sex' is the *best* I have ever used. This is the reason my eyeliner always looks so sharp. Take it from me, this eyeliner said Trans Rights Matter!

Not Everything Will Work – That's Okay

As I said earlier, some things will work out perfectly, and some things won't. This is pretty much the rhythm of life. Being totally honest, we all know what this feels like. It would be great for things to always work out perfectly, but we don't live in Richard Curtis's rom-com version of the world. So, sometimes things are just a bit shit, darling!

How you move on from what we can call life hiccups is important, though. There is an energy transfer, and if handled incorrectly then it can do some damage. Don't fret. It simply means you need to spend a little time working out what happened and where to go next.

The things that don't work out for us are not a wasted enterprise, my darling. These less successful parts of life leave space and energy for other things to work well and be a positive impact on your life. Perhaps they teach you how not to approach a task, teach you that confrontation makes things worse for you or give you a heads up that wearing skirts makes you feel uncomfortable.

You now have the introspection to go and try something different. This could be the inspiration that will lift you to new heights in your pursuit of self. I adore that this means that we don't always know what is around the corner for us – a nice way for life to surprise us!

Be happy to embrace the swings and misses of life because of this magic energy transfer that gives you an infinite amount of second chances. Trust the process of figuring yourself out and embrace the bumps in the road, darling. You've got this!

Document Your Journey

On a hard drive in the left-hand drawer of my desk I have 50,000 pictures archived from the years of content creation and the pursuit of fashion. This is my visual journey. It is so wonderful for me to look over on the days when perhaps I don't feel like the best version of myself.

I am so grateful to myself that I have this to look back on. We exist with ourselves every day. We can't always see the changes as they happen, but by documenting my visual identity like this, I have been able to see myself evolve and grow.

This is such a vital part of my identity. I urge you to document your own journey, maybe with something as simple as a selfie every time you feel really great. Or, perhaps, get a friend to launch your influencer career and spam your friends' Instagram feeds.

However you choose to document your visual identity, consider it as a healthy way of exploring your personal development.

Key Takeaways from This Chapter

- ♥ Listen to Helen Hayes: every expert was once a beginner!
- ♥ You should try things at least once, otherwise you will never know.
- ♥ Self-doubt is normal, but should be given airtime with caution.
- ♥ Don't solicit opinions from those who don't support you fully!
- ♥ Take your self-development one day at a time.
- ♥ Be happy to embrace the swings and misses of life, which will give you an infinite amount of second chances to try other things!
- ♥ Find simple ways to document your own journey.

Come Shop at the Self-Expression Supermarket

Self-expression is a simple enough concept, but when you juggle all of the things we have discussed in this chapter at once, it can be a lot to handle. Moving forwards exploring your self-expression, you will need to budget for these separate threads that pull on you.

I thought you could work out how to budget for this emotionally by shopping with me at the Self-Expression Supermarket. I've been generous and given you £6 to spend. You can spend the full amount or less than the full amount, but not a penny more. So make sure you spend it wisely and work out how to fit these elements of self-expression into your life.

Chapter 10

Connections and Allyship

As non-binary people, at one point or another, we have all experienced isolation from mainstream life and felt the pain of being pushed to the side simply for expressing who we truly are. It is important for us to foster relationships that help us feel connected but that do not drain our energy.

As we move into a life where we take space for who we truly are, the relationships we hold space for in our hearts have to work for us. Otherwise, this is just as toxic as previous encounters in our lives! It is also necessary in terms of how we can take some of the relationships we have and allow allies to form naturally. This will help create change for us as a whole.

Daily Life Can Be Hard and This Is Okay

Okay, so it's not okay that daily life is not always okay, but it will be okay! That might not be the clearest sentence I have ever written in my career, but I want to clear this up with you from the get go. You will know this yourself, as with all people. We have good days, and we have less good days!

Think of the less good days as bumps in the road. As human beings our mental ability is like suspension, and we can handle the odd bump. Obviously the bigger the bump, the harder it is to deal with. This is not unique to the non-binary community. It just feels like our road has more potholes than most. This is a job for the local council!

This book is all about positivity and joy, that is a certainty, but there are some realities that need to be explained for some of my advice to have context and purpose. I want you to know you are not alone. My words over the next few pages should help you see that.

We Have All Felt Isolation

On the whole, the public psyche holds a very distinct idea of isolation to be true – typically someone on their own for an extended period of time, sometimes portrayed in charity adverts around the festive period of Christmas. This is a valid form of isolation, but not the only one.

Existing in the world, separate from the community you belong to, is another form of isolation. Your phone probably holds a great deal of wonderful and supportive people, but they may not be around you all the time. The way we exist in very small pockets means that, for many, we are the only non-binary person we interact with on a daily basis.

We all understand what it means to feel isolated. There is obviously the narrative of queer people moving to bigger conurbations, but not all of us have the financial stability to do this, so some of us end up being isolated.

One of the most poignant things I have ever read about isolation and loneliness is that being lonely is not being alone. Loneliness is being in a room full of people and feeling alone. We can be surrounded by family or peers, but it can be very isolating being the only non-binary person.

You Don't Have to Be Strong All the Time

We're presented a very warped perception of non-binary people and the wider transgender community: we are either very strong angry activists, or we are unable to cope with the pressures of life. This is a very narrow view of us as a community, with no nuance or understanding of individuality at all. This kind of thinking drives me absolutely wild.

There is no bigger truth than the fact that we don't have to be strong all the time. We don't have to have the best day every day: it can also be a day that feels fine – nothing remarkable – just a day. This, however, doesn't diminish your strength or your resolve. The fact that you are able to show diverse emotions means that you are a perfect example of a human – imperfect by nature!

There is so much life in between 'good' and 'bad'. There is strength in exploring all forms of emotions you carry as a human, and that involves all manner of feelings each and every day on this planet. Our connection to the world can feel fraught. In itself, that means that there will be ups and downs, but this takes nothing away from your sense of self or character, and I really need you to hear this.

No Person Is an Island Entirely Unto Themselves

Growing up, I felt the isolation I have described. I thought that this was unique to me; that it was just me who had to hide who I was, avoiding attention, and that I was truly alone. Having grown up, I have seen that this is an experience countless people go through, both inside and outside the community. I want you to know that, although it may feel like it sometimes, you are not alone!

I have always felt that other people are disappointing. As relationships develop, they show you their flaws; I feel the urge to move away. Combining this with the pressures placed on me by society, it forced me to isolate myself further from peers growing up. I came to prefer my own company. This was harmful behaviour, and something I am working to move away from. From speaking to different queer people, learning to trust others is something that we all struggle with.

If this is resonates with you in any way, I would urge you to find ways to trust people. This is easier said than done, but once you let some of your barriers down, it can begin to bring light into the darker corners of your life. This may look different for each of us, but keep reading for some methods that will allow trust to develop.

How to Create Mutually Beneficial Relationships

On the road to letting more people in, and allowing yourself to trust others, we need to build mutually beneficial relationships. This not only reduces the feeling of isolation but it also gives us other things to live for. Some days we need a little more excitement than just our own thoughts.

I am sure you have all been here, but, just in case, here is an example from a relationship that is not mutually beneficial. Person A demands the presence of Person B, even though Person B has plans. B is made to drop their plans for A. When B arrives, A then pays no attention to B and wastes both their time.

Kids, this is toxic behaviour! This is something and someone you shouldn't be wasting your time on. I know. I have been there! So, this is me reminding you to seek out more for yourself. You are worth it!

Written down, it feels like I am suggesting that friendships and relationships are a lot of work. In my own experience they are! But a mutually beneficial relationship creates experiences where both parties get something out of it and brings joy or, at the very least, causes no negative emotional response.

An example of a mutually beneficial relationship is a video call where both parties speak about concerns. Both parties have time to speak about their day. Both enjoy the time they spent together. This is equal, developmental and nourishing for all involved.

The key to so much happiness is having the right people around you. Forging mutually beneficial relationships is key. It may feel for a while like you don't have this, or that you have to work out how to move away from some people. Over time, you will begin to see who is there for you. Then you can nourish that relationship for the mutual benefit it brings.

Quality Over Quantity

At school, the popular girls terrified me. I mean the ones who roamed around in big packs. They loved each other, especially on birthdays! These tight-knit cliques always perpetuated the idea that having loads of friends is the only way to be a functioning human. I cannot imagine how exhausting it was to remember all their names and to have 12-way conversations. Thankfully, I was never in such an exclusive group. However, the idea that large friendship groups are better is still perpetuated! To exist and not have that makes us feel like social pariahs!

This is my line in the sand, reader. I am here to tell you that quality over quantity is always the best approach to life and that one deep connection is better than 12 shallow ones. This leaves more room to develop meaningful connections with those around you, and, perhaps more importantly, yourself!

Education about Non-Binary Issues Isn't Your Responsibility

I spoke about this earlier in the book, but it is worth adding some context and detail for you again. The burden of education always falls on those who know the most, and as non-binary people we are seen as world gender experts. Suddenly, every time you meet someone, it is like being on sodding *Mastermind*, but this is not my specialist subject – it's just my life!

This extends to issues surrounding the wider transgender community, especially on big news days. The very day I sat to write this section, a High Court ruling affecting the transgender community was headline news. A large and influential transgender charity asked me to share their posts about this and urged me to ensure that people knew they were there to help. This interaction left me feeling a bit shaken. I hadn't seen the news. Honestly, I was a bit upset by it, and now I was being asked to spend time and effort spreading the word. In this instance I chucked a retweet and a quote tweet 20 minutes later, but I did no more.

This is very important for people to understand. It is not the job of transgender, non-binary and gender non-conforming people to speak up about these issues, especially when these issues are deeply personal and traumatic. We are not news outlets, and unless you're an actual journalist, then it is not, and never will be, your job. It *is* someone's job though, and I will tell you who the work should be done by. Carry on reading to find out.

The Importance of Allies

The role of allies is constantly downplayed in daily life. Sometimes it is seen as a choice – an option if cisgender people have the time. This couldn't be any further from the truth of the matter. Allies are not an option. They are a necessity if we are to have our identities safeguarded. The issue is that for all the education and labour we end up providing as individuals and collectively, society does not listen to us. We cannot go into spaces where we aren't safe, because we are ignored and our safety is at risk!

The missing link here is allies. Their duty is to us. All they have to do is be a little bit uncomfortable. They need to raise our concerns and raise awareness of the dangers that existing right now can carry; they need to do that in the spaces where they are readily accepted, where we may struggle, such as corporate work environments, family gatherings and public spaces like hospitals.

Putting their own comfort at risk sounds huge, but in reality it isn't! Very few things can take that comfort away from them. Allies need to pick up the slack because we cannot do all this work alone, and what's more, while we are performing labour, we are not living! That is not good enough. *We deserve better.*

If you want to help someone become a better ally, then these few tips will really help that process. Also, if a potential ally is reading this, and you have come here to learn about our life, then this is for you!

- Sharing a post on Instagram every now and then does not an ally make!
- Speak up for us, but do your research. Google the area. Make sure you are not misrepresenting the people you are trying to help.
- You are not doing this for thanks. Don't expect a pat on the back. You are doing it because you're a decent human.
- Know when to take up space but also when to hold space. Holding space allows you to give it to non-binary people so that they can be heard if they feel comfortable to do so.
- Don't do this once and then never again. We would rather you didn't bother!
- Be okay with the idea that you might get it wrong. Be prepared to actually learn with humility. We would rather have an imperfect person trying than someone who does nothing out of fear of being wrong. In short, *get it wrong*, and *move on*!
- Share this behaviour with others who could be an ally to our community. The more allies the better things could be!

♥ ♥ ♥

Understand that discomfort isn't going to kill or harm you! It is important to get used to that feeling of getting it wrong sometimes and being uncomfortable. Sit with that, and understand why you feel things in a certain way, and why you react in a certain way. This is key for me too, I know I can get defensive too, and I say I'm one of the good people! We view the world in such binary terms of good and bad people. It is because of these really rigid things that we end up tying ourselves in knots all the time.

I also would look at how you can use your privilege – whether that is time, money or power – to be able to amplify and support the people that need those things from you the most. Everyone is always tying themselves in knots because there are so many ways to be an ally! Instead, just pick one of the things that you have an abundance of. You might have lots of time, so volunteer. You might have excess cash, so you can donate. You might have an incredible network that you can mine for time and money! It is important to just start somewhere within these spaces.

♥ ♥ ♥

Nicole Ocran (she/her), digital creator and author

What Is Equality?

Equality is a word that is often batted about but perhaps is not fully understood as it is a complex and multilayered term. The need for equality stems from inequality, where people have unequal access to resources. Equality should ensure an equal access to resources but does not always make the situation any better. So, for some, equality can feel very surface deep.

One way to help is by the use of equity. This provides custom tools that identify inequality and helps fix it. True equality is actually justice, where the system has been altered to ensure that all people have both access to resources and the right tools to help access said resources.

The reason I bring this to you is that there is a lack of equal justice, especially for the non-binary community. When people say that we have made so much progress, I think what they mean is that it is easier to be white, cisgender and queer. However, there are so many intersections of minority communities that are not afforded equality. Until we *all* have equality, the world will *never be equal*.

♥ ♥ ♥

As a cisgender gay man, I believed growing up that I was the only one, and that my issues were unique. At the time it felt like I was the only one experiencing that. I had to very quickly learn that coming out as a gay man isn't the biggest issue. It is a hurdle for so many people – I don't want to take that away from anyone. There is a bigger picture here – other people also need support.

It is important to me to be an ally because as queer people there are different levels of struggle. I have dealt with what I need, in terms of finding myself and my queerness. Now it is my time to give back. I am in a position to help and support other people in our community. I must do this. Regardless of who you are, everyone needs a support network.

I set up a platform – For the Love of Queers – with the sole aim to lift the voices of the underrepresented. This provided a network for other people, it was never about me. My core values from day one were to ensure that this was a safe space.

♥ ♥ ♥

Spencer Cooper (he/him), digital creator and podcaster

The Nuanced Conversation

What is often forgotten is the nuanced duality of life, and using the term duality is also a little limiting. We can feel more than one emotion in one moment. There can be joy with sadness; there can be love with disdain. Limiting our existences to just one of suffering and pain is what has allowed so much of our experience to be erased and for the discourse to be limited to statistics and figures.

In reality, you and I both know that we're living, breathing humans, with much more variation than just sadness. I can always say that things will change, but I worry that not enough is being done about this. My work has always been focused on this kind of conversation. Yet, more needs to be done. This is where allies can step in, because they can go into spaces where they are comfortable and hold space for us.

Then, and only then, should we as people speak about our existence – when an audience is receptive to our words. There are times I speak to people about my lived experiences and what I have been through. I can see my words being ignored because it is so far removed from the experiences of the masses.

The things we have been through are not black and white – with pain there is still joy. That is something that is not being spoken about enough!

Cisgender Allies and Icons

It would be remiss not to mention that there are some wonderful cisgender icons and allies out there. They can offer inspiration for future allies!

- **Alison Hammond**
  Ms Hammond is a national treasure. She doesn't have a bad bone in her body! She has icon status in my opinion and offers light relief from some of the darker corners of the world – we must protect her at all costs!

- **Nigella Lawson**
  Now she may have a chequered past, but cooking legend Nigella Lawson is a fierce trans ally on Twitter, supporting campaigns, sharing relevant content and showing she has the ability to learn and do better in the world – we love to see it!

- **Billy Porter**
  The darling of the acting world, Porter is a tour de force when it comes to championing the rights of others, and that spans the trans community as well as the wider black LGBTQIA+ community. Through groundbreaking roles in series such as *Pose* and memorable red carpet moments, Porter is what more of the world needs.

- **The Duke and Duchess of Sussex**
  Harry and Meghan are the epitome of modern royals, whether you agree with the monarchy or not. I can't fail to mention their tireless work for the wider queer community. They're a great example of how to use a platform responsibly when you know how much influence you have.

- **Joe Lycett**
  Comedian Joe Lycett is a veritable gold mine when it comes to representation and offering diversity through his work. His

heart and joy has led him to break boundaries on shows like *The Great British Sewing Bee* and *Jo Lycett's Got Your Back*. What an icon!

- **Jameela Jamil**

  Jamil has long championed the rights of the LGBTQIA+ community and has given platform space to a plethora of trans and non-binary activists. She has taken this diverse approach to Hollywood and continues to fight our corner all over the world!

- **Lady Gaga**

  No list of allies and advocates for our community could ever be complete without the work of Ms Stefani Germanotta. From the very first breath of her career, Gaga has worked tirelessly to support the LGBTQIA+ community and continues to do so. I have no choice but to fully endorse Lady Gaga in this book!

Key Takeaways from This Chapter

- ♥ You don't have to be strong all the time.
- ♥ Ensure you have ways to trust people, to create a security buffer of like-minded people in your life.
- ♥ The key to so much happiness is having the right people around you. Forging mutually beneficial relationships is key.
- ♥ It is not the job of transgender, non-binary and gender non-conforming people to speak up about trans news stories – you are not a news desk, darling!
- ♥ The things we have been through are not black and white; embrace duality and nuance!

- ♥ If you feel able, help other people see how they can be an effective ally to our community.
- ♥ Until we *all* have equality, the world will *never be equal*.

Chapter 11

Social Media

S ocial media is probably one of the biggest changes to human life in centuries. It has gone on to shape the time and space in which we live. It has made so many things that were beyond most people's reach, such as having a platform, an audience and a presence in the world, more available than ever before.

It has evened out, what has, for decades, been a very uneven playing field. However, for non-binary people and the wider LG-BTQIA+ community, it has its pitfalls. With its presence unlikely to falter, it is important for me to make you aware of all the sides of this technology behemoth.

The Good

With all advances, there are nuanced levels of impact. The best place to start is the good impact. First and foremost, social media has the ability to connect people all over the world at all times of the day. Email was great, but an in-app conversation is so much easier to navigate. We can also meet people from all walks of life and widen our belief system thanks to the differences we all possess.

From a personal standpoint, social media has been instrumental in my own career. Through this technology I have been able to carve out a corner of the internet that helps people. Social media has even had a large part to play in this very book!

I spoke about the increase of visibility earlier, but we, as a community, can connect and see each other so much more than ever before. This kind of visibility is invaluable and will have changed so many people's lives. So we can all be thankful for social media in that respect. Sadly, with any good, inevitably there is bad!

The Bad

One of the best parts of social media is its unifying ability, which means all have a voice and a platform from which to share their thoughts. However, this can cause many issues. People who have deeply offensive thoughts and opinions come into our safe spaces and spread their darkness. It has become such a kick for some people that they actively seek out the platforms of the marginalized to spread this hatred.

It is easy to deal with now and then, but some of us in the community who are more active online deal with this daily. I struggle to post without attracting attention I would rather not deal with. There are so many times I don't feel I can speak my mind in order not to offend anyone, yet others are not so conscientious.

This shit show is one of the reasons social media no longer feels fun, or, at times, safe.

The Ugly

It will come as no surprise to you, but the thoughts and feelings that some choose to share on our platforms can actually get worse!

Death threats and incitement of violence have sadly become a normal part of being active online. I am not the only non-binary person this has happened to – so many people I know have faced this. It is not just in our community. It is a systemic problem.

I worried that this wasn't the right thing to share with you, as this book is supposed to be about the joy of being us. However, as I mentioned earlier, there can be more than one emotion at play in any given moment. It is also very important to me that you are in possession of all the facts. To underinform you would be to do you a disservice.

♥ ♥ ♥

When we talk about the hate that we can get online, I have re-alized in the moments it has happened to me, that while it feels very personal because they are talking about us – whatever we did or said in a post – it is really important to remember that it is not personal! I've noticed a lot of the times when someone leaves a hate comment it is the other person behind a screen revealing their own feelings and issues.

They are using you as a gateway to express themselves. Do I think it is fair for them to do this? No, I don't, but at the end of the day, I remind myself that these are people who are hurting and need to express this in some way. This allows me to detach myself because the comment is not about me, it is their issues that they need to work through, so it bothers me less.

Social media is very important for non-binary people – do we even exist in the media outside of social media? We don't! I'm not sure I have seen a non-binary character on television, maybe Drag Race was the first and only time. Social media is the only place where I find people that represent us. I can find people that I relate to and connect with. It is important because a lot of the people who never had a voice in our society are now able to have their voice heard, and feel valid.

♥ ♥ ♥

Manuel Santos (they/them), social media icon

Influencers and Activism

As with all new media, it doesn't take long before someone figures out how to make money from it. The rise of influencers and activism has reached an all-time high. There are days where we can see nothing but #ads and paid partnerships.

This is not a problem per se. It has created a grey area when it comes to the amount of power individuals have been given. The rise of influencers has placed a lot of importance on a select few. This of course has ramifications, as their life experiences differ greatly from the people they are supposed to be representing.

It has made it harder to have work taken seriously. Brands only work with commercial interests. This has affected the LGBTQIA+ community and has also impacted non-binary people in ways that are becoming quite toxic.

Toxic Activism

Toxic activism is the misuse of activism. Essentially, it is poor behaviours disguised as activism, which sets back positive momentum, and is *rife* in the LGBTQIA+ community. If you have interacted with the community online, I think you will all have seen some questionable behaviour.

I am outlining what this behaviour looks like so you can spot it and know which outlets are possibly not helpful for you on your journey with your identity. Keep reading to find out some of the things that need to stop.

Calling Fellow Activists Out

We all make mistakes. It's part of being human, but there is no need to initiate a witch-hunt. I discussed earlier how we have supposedly moved on from this behaviour. It is the twenty-first century after all! Calling out is part of the toxic side of cancel culture, which is a different chapter and book all together. As I said earlier, the landscape of social media has provided millions, if not billions, of people the ability to share how they feel, which is wonderful, but it can get out of hand.

I think there is a very necessary place for accountability. People should be able to help others learn, but calling people out publicly is not the right way to do this! Instead, I fully endorse *calling in* people who have made a mistake.

'Calling in' is having the conversation but doing so in private! Send an email, a direct message, pick up the phone and speak to that person. Let them know your issues, and help them learn. Also, be prepared for them to help you learn too! None of us is infallible. We're all human, with feelings, and deserve to be treated accordingly.

Believing They're *Always* Right

No single person has all the answers. No one activist has all the answers! One of the best parts of being online is that we can learn from the whole community. Yet there has been an unequal amount of power handed to certain voices in the community. This causes issues for us all.

Toxic activism exists in a space that promotes the idea that a handful of activists are the answer to all our problems. These are the only people we need to listen to, apparently! We actually need to hear from a diverse range of people. I hope that as we move forwards, we can begin to see the need for more diversity and inclusion in all areas of media, especially in the digital world of social media.

Virtue Signalling

This is when a person shares work and opinions in a visual display of allyship, but under the surface there is nothing else being done. It is getting harder and harder to spot this kind of behaviour as more and more people create 'resources' that are just hot takes and not actually helpful.

This behaviour is not backed up by resources and does not go to any effort to actually change the things it purports to condemn.

Virtue signalling takes up space in feeds and prevents real activism from reaching its audience. We all saw examples of feed jamming with the black square issues for the Black Lives Matter movement back in the summer of 2020. It is just another area of online behaviour of which we have to be cautious.

Gatekeeping

Gatekeeping is intrinsic to toxic activism. Together, they help each other out cyclically. Essentially, this is certain individuals being the voice of a community. Their voice is the only one allies hear and listen to.

Allies and wider society base their opinion of that community solely on that one person, which plays a part in erasing experiences. This may not seem to be an issue, but it is tricky if expectations are then placed on other people. Gatekeeping only benefits a few. Typically, in the LGBTQIA+ community, this is cisgender, thin, able-bodied and white activists. How often have we as gender diverse people seen this play out time and time again?

We have the power to spot this happening and say something about it. Big corporations and platforms have a responsibility to be diverse. We can always call them in, or push allies to do this on our behalf. It is their job after all!

So How Do We Fix This?

The wider community needs to be listening to a diverse range of voices to ensure they have a well-rounded, experience-filled version of a topic! We all need to be sharing diverse voices allowing others to see different sources of information, calling people in when they make mistakes and making activism inclusive, not an exclusive club run by a small number of people.

The LGBTQIA+ community has come a long way but is being choked by toxic activism from the inside. We need to hold this accountable in a conflict-free way. This is about *growth for all of us* after all.

Key Takeaways from This Chapter

- ♥ Social media has good sides and bad sides – be aware of this!
- ♥ Social media, however, does have a very important role to play in representation for non-binary people.
- ♥ Curate the spaces you interact with online – remember you can block harmful accounts!
- ♥ Call people in when they make a mistake – we can all still learn!
- ♥ Be aware of how to spot virtue signalling and gatekeeping – these are not helping our cause.
- ♥ We should all be striving for diversity online, as this will help more people.
- ♥ Always stay safe online, and if you don't feel comfortable, remember you can leave the space!

Social Media Guess Who

To see if you have worked out what behaviour you want to avoid online, let's explore some profiles, and you can decide if you want to swipe right on their behaviour or swipe left and send them a swift call-in email...

SOCIAL MEDIA WHO'S WHO

STEVE
he/him

LOVES: Ski breaks and LADS!
HATES: Green juice
ONLINE ACTIVITY: Shares lots of affirmations and quotes daily but only posts topless pictures on his grid. Only ever shares work from creators he fancies and never does anything else!

OTTO
they/them

LOVES: Frogs, memes & cheese
HATES: Marmite & FaceTime
ONLINE ACTIVITY: Sends direct messages to creators to let them know about issues they may have made and always leaves room for diversity and inclusivity in their feed.

KIT
they/them

LOVES: Long walks and sarcasm
HATES: Dentists & kale
ONLINE ACTIVITY: Only shares a few queer activists' work, and only because they are friends. Never shows up to protests, can't be bothered to share petitions and hates Pride.

JANE
she/her

LOVES: Documentaries
HATES: 'Woke people'
ONLINE ACTIVITY: Posts hot takes every day and loves to cancel people. NEVER makes mistakes #perfect! Only loves mainstream brands and influencers and loves to promote fast fashion #ad!

Chapter 12

The Gift of Time

The media presents us with the idea that in order to be valid, we have to be complete people. In essence, we need to have finished exploring our identities and present the fixed version of ourselves. I feel like this is a perfect time to debunk this myth.

It would be wonderful to snap your fingers and have all your ducks in a row, but life is not like that. It is wise be open-minded about the timelines of your life and those of others.

Not One of Us Is the Complete Article

When we look at role models, we mistakenly see them as neatly packaged human beings, fully formed and perfect. Life is not about growing and developing to a fixed point. Life doesn't just take care of itself when you reach a certain level.

In order to stay at the level they're at, role models are treading water. That is to say, they are constantly working to be that person. We can extrapolate that to ourselves, seeing our developing gender identity and the relationship we have with that as a constant process.

As comfortable and happy as I am within myself right now, I know that I am on a path that is evolving. Employing the tactics of documenting your journey that I discussed earlier is a great way to see how this plays out daily.

Perfection Takes Years; Have Patience

I wasn't a fan of school. There are some systematic lessons we can lift from the learning institute that formed much of what we all know today. In the UK we study subjects like English, maths and science for 12 years, and some can go on to do a further two years of A levels, and then perhaps even take a degree, a Master's and finally a PhD.

Learning takes decades. We accept that when it comes to subjects like maths. However, when it comes to personal development, we want it to happen overnight. This is a very silly way to approach our own development. Twelve years of maths very quickly left my mind, and even with another 12, I still wouldn't be able to do long division! But imagine how far your sense of self will have come in 12 years, as long as you give it the time it needs, darling! Give yourself the patience you require, because we're all in it for the long haul.

If Something Is Worth It, It Is Worthy of Your Time

Small tasks can be put to bed in a short amount of time. Classic examples of this are making the bed, posting a letter or eating a bowl of cereal. Medium tasks – yes, you've guessed it – take more time to achieve. This is very simplistic, descriptive work here, but it is a poignant reminder that time is important.

The assumption of self and the adaptation of your full truth and identity is something that is worth effort. This is a very large task. It requires concentration and effort. If this process is worth it to you, and you want to reach a sense of self that fully fits you inside and out, then *it is worthy of your time*.

Posting a letter doesn't take years. We don't have to devote much time to it! Figuring out who you are is a constant and ever-changing process that is worthy of a great deal of time, so award it to yourself!

Be Ambitious But Be Realistic

One of the landmark additions to my own life was the application of makeup. Combining makeup with continuous exploration of my gender identity, has been such a fortuitous pairing and is now a true passion. When I first picked up a makeup brush I knew that I had it in me to achieve great things with that tool but that it would not be straight away.

By placing that realistic expectation on myself, I was happy to take my time developing my skills and honing the application process into the decent job I perform on my face right now. This is applicable to all areas of development. Pure ambition is necessary in this magical equation because it becomes the driving force that helps you improve and gives you reason to perfect your development, but *you* also need time.

By having no time constraints or boundaries, you provide yourself a caring and compassionate environment to give yourself space to flourish. They say that diamonds are formed under pressure, but did you know that very pressure can cause that stone to explode from the inside out when it is polished? So, perhaps, allowing beauty to blossom over time is a far healthier approach. After all, I would like you all to stay completely intact!

Rome Wasn't Built in a Day

'Rome wasn't built in a day' is an adage that is attributed to playwright John Haywood, who wrote poems, plays and proverbs in the sixteenth century. He is best known for this phrase, which implies that great things take time to build. It is simple when you think about it, yet there is more that we can take from this.

We leave John with his simple little saying, but we can find a deeper meaning. It is clear that Rome symbolizes a grand achievement. That is doubtless. We have to work constantly to achieve this end goal. Time is not the only thing necessary for the development of wonderful things. We need to employ effort and work daily in the pursuit of personal growth.

In the context of Rome, this is mosaic floors, the Colosseum and countless straight roads. I'm pretty sure you are not a series of buildings, but instead you're a developing human being. So, in the context of you, effort and work are attributed to character development – working on creating mutually beneficial relationships and strengthening the bond you have with your own sense of self.

It is pertinent to remind you that these are things you do daily anyway and require no further exertion. This is life, not a marathon, darling! Old sayings are chucked about all the time, but if we don't stop to take the time to fully understand their meaning, then they are worthless. I hope you can see the magic of a refined meaning to 'Rome wasn't built in a day' and use this in your self-development.

Good Things Come to Those Who Wait

While we are on the topic of adages that get used as little nuggets of advice, I would like to shine a light on the flawed 'good things come to those who wait'. The unfairness of this statement is ridiculous and it is the worst advice you can give anyone. So, I won't!

The statement implies that all you have to do in life is wait and wonderful things will be dropped into your lap. I am of course being very literal with this, but it is stupid and I will tell you why. In the context of marginalized communities, there are very few good-news days. We are not granted large, sweeping justices. We could wait a decade for a monumental positive change. Just to be clear, waiting for good things is preposterously bad advice.

I have laid out why it is important to give your self-development time, but it is apparent that this is not a passive passage of time, and I don't want you to be derailed by the poor guidance that 'good things come to those who wait' offers. So know that good things could come, but most of the time good things come after lots and lots of development!

Growing Pains Are Real

When we look at role models, who we have discovered are tread- ing water to maintain their progress, we assume that the path to

THE GIFT OF TIME

where they are right now was plain sailing. Surprise! Yet again we are tripping over some dangerous assumptions. 'Dangerous' is an alarming word, but I use it here to highlight how much harm you can do to yourself by assuming something is fact without taking in the full truth and reality.

Growing pains happen in the legs of children as their bodies adjust to strenuous activities and have no links to growth spurts or muscles stretching. I failed my biology A levels systematically, resat every single exam and scraped a D, so my knowledge of human biology is shaky at best, but growing pains aren't a real thing physically. The mental strain of developing and growing into yourself is real, and I would argue that these growing pains are real. When we use someone else's journey as a reason to feel we are behind, we are making a mistake because we have only seen a very small part of that journey. We have not seen all the hurdles they have faced.

The process from where you started to where you are today has not always been easy, and that is a given for all of us! The next chapters in your story will also have some discomfort. My words are here to provide you with a sense of preparedness that will help you overcome this.

Stop on a Landing

Throughout this section, we have discussed themes of time and continuous levels of effort. When laid out like this, life can feel like a set of stairs that go on forever. We are supposed to climb those stairs every day. We climb those stairs to broaden our horizons, to improve our skills and to reach higher standards.

When we are in the right mindset, these stairs are not too strenuous. It is the daily rhythm of life. However, climbing for climbing's sake can become very tiring. Before long the process of life can become exhausting. To be clear, it is not progress to submit to things that don't help you; it is actually emotional strain. There is merit to putting constant toil on pause sometimes.

I have always been a fan of *Changing Rooms*, and naff DIY has a special place in my heart. If you want to lose hours, ask me to talk about Linda Barker's teapot disaster! With this somewhat tenuous link where I squeeze another vestige of my personality into these pages, I would like to do some improvements to your staircase and build some landings for you.

Adding landings to your stairs allows you to take breaks, giving you the space to catch your breath and live a little in one place. Allowing routines that form the basis of your life to keep you going gives you the space to settle into your life and enjoy it in the moment. Stopping on the landings when you need to also allows you perspective. You can look down at your past easily in a safe, reflective way.

We can just exist and not be working all the time. It is so important to know this. It is not said often enough, my darlings, so take this as a hearty reminder!

Look Back at How Far You Have Come

One of the glorious things about time is that, whatever happens, a new day will always come. Nothing can stop that. Even without being conscious, our lives progress every minute of every day. Even though you might not feel you have achieved anything, things are always happening!

The end of this chapter is a very good place to remind you to look back at just how far you have come. It will blow your mind!

Allow it to remind you to have faith in the processes of being human. It also provides the foundations of contentment moving forwards, because it allows you to think that you will have grown and evolved in 18 months, even if this is not a conscious decision.

Knowing that you are on a continuous path should offer you solace and comfort on darker days. It can also delight you on brighter days. Life is not like elastic. You won't suddenly ping back to where you were three years ago. It might not always feel like it, but we're always on the move, even when we stop on a landing, and this direction is exactly where you are supposed to be going.

There is no need to force anything. Don't go on a huge process to alter who you are. You are wonderful each and every day you are on this planet, my darling.

♥ ♥ ♥

I've had to do work like a pinball machine in terms of gender – being a tomboy as a child, trying to find femininity as a teenager, and it not feeling quite right. Then rushing headfirst into masculinity, completely closing the door on femininity. Now I am open to anything. People experience this process in many ways, and not just with gender. It takes time, it feels incredibly fast, because it is a constant, but it does take time.

I have let go of a need for answers, and that is exciting to me. I am someone who loves to ask questions, but I've been able to let go of the need for answers to all the questions! That is a clear lesson I can trace back to my experience of gender.

I have a visceral experience of an ever-evolving self, I've seen it in myself, I have felt the constant change. That is inherently exciting because you have no idea who you're going to be. Letting go of a need for control in a way lets you feel more stable. I don't need the control that provides answers. Now that I have let go of that, I feel more stable in the present. I feel like I am more present, because of that arrival at a solidity in unknowability. It is incredibly exciting because you are just finding new ways to be yourself.

♥ ♥ ♥

Thymian Gadd (they/them), writer and artist

The Dinner Party Question

I haven't been to many dinner parties myself. I always assumed I would tackle them when I blossom into a 'proper adult', but I do love to discuss who people's ideal dinner party guests would be. You can pick anyone from time, living or not. How exciting! I would pick Princess Diana, Alison Hammond and Freddie Mercury – what a fab night that would be!

Anyway, back to the gift of time, to sum up this chapter. I thought I would pose a similar question to you, and you can only pick one or the other. Would you rather have an intimate dinner party with yourself from somewhere in the future, or have a dinner party with two of your past selves from your timeline?

One would answer some of your burning questions about your future, and the others would allow you to see just how far you have come! The choice is yours, but it starts a wonderful conversation about the gift of time and who you have become and who you will be, so take the time to think this over.

Key Takeaways from This Chapter

- ♥ We are not the complete article – we are always evolving.
- ♥ Patience is your friend – it is okay that some things take longer than you want!
- ♥ Figuring out who you are is a constant and ever-changing process that is worthy of a great deal of time, so award it to yourself!
- ♥ Always remember that Rome was not built in a day, darling.
- ♥ Most times good things come after lots and lots of development, so devote some time to yourself.

💜 We can just exist and not be working all the time. It is so important to know this.

💜 Remember to look just how far you have come!

Chapter 13

Distractions

Throughout these pages no one could accuse me of presenting a falsehood. I hope that my reality-focused words have gently highlighted some of the truths we face in the non-binary community. To continue in this vein, it is important to look at the things we need on the days where things are just okay, or perhaps less than okay.

The natural undulations of life mean that some days a spanner can be thrown into the works. Whether we are dealing with things done by others or our own mental health, we all need to take time for ourselves. We all have good days and dark days. For non-binary people, dark days can pull our emotional levels down to a point where we really need to pause and heal. This chapter will offer respite for overstretched readers.

Health Is Wealth

Honestly, typing that statement, even I rolled my eyes. Only wealth is wealth. I recently saw a therapist say that most people would benefit from therapy, but in reality, most people could do with a little bit more money; however, that is a conversation for another book! Back to our actual health. Basic health is an important part of our lives. There are key parts that we can focus on to ease the effects of outside pressures. Stress and anxiety build up throughout the day, and our ability to deal with this is greatly affected by three key things:

- **Water**

    This is quite literally a hydration check. Have you been drinking enough? You know the right amount of fluids for you, because we have all been dehydrated. Keeping your fluid levels up is so important.

    Not only does it make all your bodily functions work well, but it also helps with your sleep levels and keeps your skin healthy. Great sleep and happy skin are worth drinking a few more glasses of water for, right?

- **Sleep**

    We all know that sleep is important. It allows many of the healing functions of the body to take place. Sleep is elusive for many of us, and the pressure to sleep can be very daunting. To help ensure you get the most out of the sleep you can get, try to wind down before you sleep, reducing screen time before that can take place, and making the environment that you sleep in as comfortable as possible.

    It is hard when many people live, work and relax in the same room that they sleep in, and maintaining boundaries can be hard, but sleep should always come first!

- **Balance**

    As with all things, too much is, well, too much. Having a balance of all the factors you need to keep yourself well is key. This looks very different for each of us, and only *you* will know what works for *you*. Keeping sleep/food/exercise diaries can help you keep track of what does and doesn't work for your body and can be a great place to start when looking for a way to bring more balance to your life.

The Power of Nostalgia

Nostalgia is a personal favourite of mine, and for a long time I assumed incorrectly that it was my fear of letting the past go that meant I clung to nostalgia. I have since realized that nostalgia is a thing of comfort because it can quieten the noise around us.

Nostalgia to me is like a very well-worn item of clothing. You are familiar with each other. It fits and knows your body, and there is comfort in this familiarity. When you wear that garment you don't have to adjust it. It feels like second nature to you and offers no resistance to your day.

Just like your favourite jumper or dressing gown, nostalgia is the things we can access from our past when our present is a little overwhelming. This can be things from our childhood, passions past or even just a favourite film you enjoyed a decade ago.

Understanding that nostalgia is soul food is very healthy. When it comes to distractions from the world around you, it is a very healthy asset to have in your arsenal against the world.

Ways to Forget About the World

The world has this very annoying habit of constantly turning, so, no matter your mood, things will continue with a pace that makes some days feel very hectic. When it comes to distraction, trying to forget about the world just for an afternoon can have many benefits, namely, that you can focus on yourself and create some space and time to recover.

Yet the world is a noisy place. How can we reduce the volume to allow ourselves the space to have some time for ourselves? Well, there are a few methods that have offered me solace in the past that might work for you.

- **Turn your phone off**

  Simply put, cutting your very present digital connection to the world can offer solace and comfort. It can take a while to disconnect. The first time you do it you might even feel a little lost. However, taking away the constant updates and bad news provides you some space that allows you to think and hear your own thoughts.

- **A change of scenery**

  If you have been staring at the same four walls for a while, then they may begin to feel oppressive. I don't know if you have seen the film *Muppet Treasure Island*? It's an adaptation of Robert Louis Stevenson's novel *Treasure Island*. There is one specific scene when the boat has been at sea for six weeks. There has been no wind for five days, and the lack of activity or change causes the crew to contract cabin fever. Google it. It's a very catchy song. I have used this tenuous link to explain that seeing the same environment, day in, day out, can affect our mood. So a change can be a good thing.

- **Fresh air**

  Fresh air can be just the thing when you are looking for a

change of scenery. Go for a walk, long or short, it really doesn't matter, but just getting out of your living space and breathing different air can be the thing that you need to shake up your day. It can be the thing that offers you the perspective that you need. It can renew your opinion on the day at hand. It may be simple, but it is also mightily effective!

- **A personal moment of joy**

  It is so important to find that one thing that you do for no reason other than the pure joy it brings you. For me this is having a gorgeous scented candle in my office that makes working more of a pleasure. There is no real need for it. It serves no purpose other than to make me smile, but that is reason enough. Try to find a personal moment of joy, my darling!

♥　♥　♥

Self-enquiry through art practice can look like anything, it doesn't need to be self-portraiture, it can be writing, or collaging, as it's about how you analyse and reflect upon it. It is research, and it is therapy. This way you can then be more reflexive in your thinking. Sometimes we can think too much and the act of making artwork can take you into a different headspace.

If you zone into the process, and cut off the thinker, you can produce something and then look at it and reflect upon what is there, as opposed to being caught in a negative thinking spiral, but instead be reflexive to and with your thinker. That is the power and the relief that making has, being able to go back and look at work when I am questioning my identity again, or not feeling confident or like I am making stuff up, or it's not real, all those kinds of self-doubt.

There is an empowerment and strength in making that is unique. I can look at my work and understand that this is my expression and experience, it is beautiful, difficult, complicated but it is solely mine and only I could have made it.

♥　♥　♥

Lo Lo No (they/them), artist and curator

Ten Ways to Enjoy Today

Do you want to have a truly great day today or tomorrow? Here is a list of ten things that could work for you!

1. Have a lie in – don't set an alarm – commitments permitting.
2. If organization is your thing, move your living space around, or sort out your sock drawer!
3. Find other non-binary people on Instagram and make a new friend!
4. Try a new recipe for dinner. Who knows, it could become your signature dish!
5. See my list of iconic films to watch in a few pages' time.
6. Find a new hobby. I have always wanted to learn how to play chess...
7. Listen to ABBA. Seriously, the most endorphin-laced music out there!
8. Have a nap, because more sleep is always a good thing.
9. Plan your next special day. Who fancies a picnic next weekend?
10. Do something for future you, anything that will save you some time, or just make you smile when you need it!

Methods of Mindfulness (Public and Private)

Mindfulness is the practice of taking more notice of your present, the way you feel and the things around you in your immediate vicinity. It is derived from Buddhism and, whether you are spiritual or not, it has a high value of efficacy. Using simple breathing techniques and methods to focus your mind, mindfulness can provide you with a healthy distraction right now.

Box breathing

For a quick reset any time, any place, to centre your breathing, use my favourite anxiety-busting method that will take you 12 seconds. With your back supported and your feet firmly on the floor, close your eyes. Breathe through your nose steadily for four seconds, making sure you feel your chest expand. Hold this breath for four seconds. Let your mind go blank. Then, slowly, exhale this breath through your mouth for four seconds. Repeat this twice more.

Simple repetitive tasks

Tasks such as colouring, jigsaw puzzles and household jobs like ironing can all have a mind-numbing effect. This is very useful when you are distracted while trying to be productive. It can also be a great way to reduce stress by allowing your mind to mull over issues naturally without overthinking.

Meditation

Meditation is a simple way to ground yourself and works well in private, in a place where you feel very comfortable. There are so many free apps, YouTube videos and blogs that offer you techniques to allow you to calm and centre yourself in the moment. I use it to help me fall asleep, it is that relaxing.

Iconic Films to Boost Your Mood

This falls into the category of nostalgia, but when it comes to a nice dose of distraction, you cannot beat a good film. Spending an hour or two doing nothing else, and without scrolling on your phone, can be just the ticket. So, if you fancy a bit of nostalgic screen time after you finish this chapter, buckle in for some iconic films to boost your mood.

- *Wallace and Gromit* – nothing says calm and content like *Wallace and Gromit*.
- *Legally Blonde* – like writing a book is hard?!
- *Working Girl* – Sigourney Weaver is sensational in this 80s classic!
- *Charlie's Angels* – Drew Barrymore created one of the most iconic reboots. Pure, feel-good fun.
- *Charlie's Angels: Full Throttle* – see above.
- *Matilda* – we support icons who love to read.
- *Aladdin* – I want nothing to do with the remake, only the Robin Williams one will do!
- *The Devil Wears Prada* – Andy's friends and partner are the real villains!
- *Death Becomes Her* – a divisive black comedy. Meryl Streep and Goldie Hawn sizzle in this film.

- *The Witches of Eastwick* – Cher, Susan Sarandon and Michelle Pfeiffer – need I say more?!

Self-Care Savours

Self-care gets a bad rep, and that's because many don't take the need for it seriously. I think on a surface level perhaps some of the actions I have listed below could be perceived as pointless. However, when done under the introspection of self, self-care can have a deeper meaning.

Introspection is a process of experiencing the world through your own feelings and emotions. When applied to self-care, suddenly frivolous activities can lead to a deeper healing process. This should all be done at your own pace, in a way that makes you feel the best. These techniques are not a quick fix, and you should allow time to adjust to these helpful suggestions.

For some of my favourite self-care saviours, keep reading...

- **Pick something you love**
  There is never enough self-fulfilling joy in life, and when it comes to self-care, giving yourself the time you need to do something you love can really boost your mood and combat levels of stress caused by others. Call a friend, build your dream home on *The Sims*, listen to music or just cook a meal. Whatever you enjoy, bring it into your self-care arsenal.

- **Time away**
  Similar to one of my pleasure presets, carving out a set amount of time each day just for you is a key way to give back to yourself. I give myself 60–90 minutes a day for a bath; that allows

me to unwind. I pop on a show and turn my phone off, and that moment truly alone allows the noise of the day to subside and gives my head the space to truly rest.

- **Routines**
  I love routines, as they are something to fall back on at times when we can't fathom up from down. Whether this be a Su-doku a day, or a step-by-step heavy skincare set-up, whatever you choose to do, it will offer you nourishment as it helps you feel balanced.

- **Try something new**
  Just as routines are super helpful to keep you balanced and grounded, trying new things has also been proven effective in boosting your self-worth. The instant challenge of a new skill, language or habit brings a small amount of difference and a purpose that can flourish without any added stress.

- **Nature can nurture you**
  I have spoken at length about the benefit of fresh air and being outside, but you can also bring this benefit inside too. Having plants and living things in your environment can improve your mood and lower your stress levels. It also has the added ben-efit of being right there when you don't want to interact with people!

♥   ♥   ♥

If I have had a hard day, the next morning I might think about how I want that day to start. If I start my day with music it is going to be a better day. You are setting the tone, allowing music to set the mood rather than anything else. I play music loud in the shower, and it makes me feel like I have got this! Singing along is also really powerful. At the end of an hour of singing out loud, you have done so much breathing and it is good for you. It is a really good way to get the circulation going!

Self-care for me is logging off. I like to take a very long walk, just listening to one album. Everything is pulling at your attention these days, so sitting and considering a whole LP is a very different thing than just listening to a playlist on shuffle. It is a great way to take in one piece of art or work that someone put together in that way specifically so that you hear it in that way.

Even if I felt rubbish, I just go out and listen to one or two albums, and when I come back I usually feel a whole lot better. Having music on and just walking leaves me with space to think. It is very therapeutic – instead of writing it down, or talking it through with someone, I can just work through my thoughts. I am doing something else whilst walking and I don't feel like I have wasted my time.

♥   ♥   ♥

Xandice Armah (they/them), DJ and creator

Key Takeaways from This Chapter

- ♥ Basic health is an important part of our lives, but balance is key!
- ♥ Nostalgia is soul food – allow it to envelop you in a warm hug to distract you.
- ♥ Find ways to shut the wider world out for a little bit to give you some calm.
- ♥ Self-care is important – remembering some of these actions can help push you through day to day.
- ♥ Hobbies are important to keep a balance of pleasure in our lives.
- ♥ Never forget the powerful effect of nature on your mood and health.
- ♥ Find out methods of coping that work for you, even if they aren't typical!

Distractions Word Search

There has been a lot of advice in this chapter, so I thought a great way to allow some of these conversations to ruminate is a word search. So dive in and see what you can find to help you distract yourself!

```
p a n t a m j g n b p o v r k v u o a b
g x q w a t e r l p l a n f t f o n b w
f b m j e d i s t u o z e r u t a n m a
p d s e u a t n e t n o c c i z x d j l
q e u r j n k c n b k z s k d c j b a l
h z e c l m d e o l z v y c i o a y i a
z i n l w a w u r e p e t i t i o n g c
p n o x s m i s l c p s s i d e r m l e
u a i e d i s t r a c t i o n e h u a q
v g t h v v f t z o t k y o j n b k t a
j r c x f m r u g e k i w u v i c d s r
c o e o w o i m t r h y o z u t n d o g
h q p d f j x i a m o e k n s u y x n y
f o s m k g p b e n b m a l s o e b n v
t v o m v s b d m r b h i l u r k v d d
x c r m e a i h e q i u s t t x o o l w
w j t r a t j x c l e z h g s h s p g u
m x n n a w h d b f s a e r a c f l e s
i w i t v z x g n i h t a e r b e b v q
l h e h s z j z e c n a l a b l u m y z
```

abba balance bed breathing comfort content distraction gromit
health hobbies introspection joy meditate mood nap nature
nostalgia organize outside plan repetition respite routine
selfcare sleep undulations wallace water

Chapter 14

Resources

t is important to me that this book acknowledges that it can only do so much. I do not have all the answers. Through the book I have explored research and other people's lives to help me bring you a well-rounded view of the world that we live in.

There is a dangerous behaviour in our community and wider society of offering up individuals as the answer to all our problems. Well, I don't believe in this kind of thinking. There is a phrase 'it takes a village to raise a child', which is a proverb suggesting that a child needs to interact with a whole community to become a well-rounded and adjusted person. In this context, I would say that it takes a village to support queer people.

If the conversations we have had in these pages have unearthed more questions, then this section is here for that. I want to sign-post places for you to go if you need more help, and when to seek external advice, and where to go to gain a full awareness of the whole LGBTQIA+ community that exists outside these pages and my humble words.

LGBTQIA+ Icons to Follow

We could always do with more inspiration in our lives, so here are some icons to bring you queer joy, darling – including all the angels who shared their thoughts with you throughout the chapters! Follow them on Instagram (or whatever social media you love) and feel as grateful as I am to have them in our world!

- **Jake Hall**
  @jsh2103 (they/them), writer and author. Jake's writing and perspective are incredible, and they are a talent that you must follow.

- **Wednesday Holmes**
  @hellomynameiswednesday (they/them), artist and illustrator. Wednesday is a tour de force and is the main reason I got involved in the realm of activism. They have supported my career for years, and they do so much for our community.

- **Az Franco**
  @youcancallmeaz (he/him), artist and activist. Az is an icon when it comes to online activism and creating content that will cause change.

- **Grace Shush**
  @graceshushh (they/them), drag artist. Shush uses drag to boost our moods and is one half of Thicc London, a queer body-positive club night.

- **Lexi Chandra**
  @iamlexchandra (she/they), writer and model. Lexi injects such a vivacious energy into the world, and I have personally learnt so much from them. They're a *must*-follow, my angels!

- **Darkwah Kyei-Darkwah**
  @hausofdarkwah (they/them), art director, writer and pre-senter. Darkwah is a true icon and is showing the world how to rule the world through the intersection of race and their gender identity.

- **Jordan Benedetti**
  @enbyjordan (they/them), activist, speaker and artist. Jordan educates in a way that brings an audience in and creates actual change in such a beautiful way.

- **Shiva Raichandani**
  @shivaraichandani (he/they), performance artist and director. Shiva uses dance as a form of storytelling. They have featured on *Britain's*, *India's* and *France's Got Talent* and are so talented!

- **Nicole Ocran**
  @nicoleocran (she/her), digital creator and author. Nicole is a staunch ally to the LGBTQIA+ community and happens to be one of the loveliest people on the internet. An ally who must be followed!

- **Spencer Cooper**
  @lovequeers/@spencooper (he/him), photographer and founder of For the Love of Queers. Spencer is one of the biggest cheerleaders for all queer people. His platform holds space for people across the spectrum of the whole community.

- **Manuel Santos**
  @themanuelsantos (they/them), social media icon. TikTok star

and self-proclaimed Holy Trinity, Manuel is hilarious, intelligent and an incredible content creator!

- **Thymian Gadd**
@thymian_gadd (they/them), artist and writer. Thymian has some of the most succinct ways of contextualizing feelings that change the way I see the world; they're such an icon.

- **Lo Lo No**
@lo_lo_no_ (they/them), artist and curator. Arts curator for Margate Pride in the UK, artist, academic icon and former fashion designer, Lo Lo No has a thought-provoking view of the world we can all learn from.

- **Xandice Armah**
@xz_dice (they/them), DJ and creator. Xandice is a DJ and co-founder of the queer party for women, trans and non-binary folks Gal Pals.

- **Sheerah Ravindren**
@sheerahr (she/they), model and activist. Sheerah refers to themselves as a creative with a moral obligation and does such an amazing job – a must-follow.

- **Jacob Edwards**
@itsjacobedward (they/them), radio host and campaigner for representation in radio. Jacob is such a trailblazer. They were the first non-binary presenter on Radio 1. They inspire me so much.

- **Joshua Allen**
  @joshuaobawole (they/them), artist, writer, speaker and founder of Black Excellence Collective. They send positive energy through the internet that is so warm and affirming.

- **Tanya Compas**
  @tanyacompas (she/her), youth worker and campaigner. Tanya works tirelessly for the black queer community and makes such a difference to so many lives.

- **Ugla Stefanía**
  @uglastefania (they/them), trans activist, educator, author and filmmaker. Ugla is one of our community's hardest workers. They have campaigned for trans rights for over a decade.

- **Mia Violet**
  @ohmiagod (she/her), trans author and mental health activist. Mia is so successful as she channels many intersections in her work and is such a light in this world.

- **Dr Ronx Ikharia**
  @dr_ronx (they/them), trans, non-binary, A&E doctor. Dr Ronx is everything we need in modern healthcare. They educate in all that they do and give me faith that the services we access are beginning to adapt to the lives we live.

- **Char Bailey**
  @char_bailey_ (she/her), personal and business motivational coach. I had the pleasure of taking part in a breathing session run by Char and she brought a calm that I have never had

and I hope to recapture. Char is a breath of fresh air and a must-follow.

- **Bimini Bon Boulash**
  @biminibabes (they/them), drag icon, model and blonde bombshell. Bimini is doing some amazing work boosting visibility and understanding for all non-binary people – we are very lucky to have them.

- **Jeffrey Marsh**
  @thejeffreymarsh (they/them), bestselling author, social media star and personal role model. Jeffrey was one of the first non-binary people I saw thriving and showing the world how amazing we are. A huge star in our community!

How to Speak Up about Mental Health

Isn't it strange – and I could be alone on this one – that we all know when we are less than okay, but we find it so hard to vocalize this? I have spent many years in the past holding onto my feelings and not giving truthful answers to enquiries after my health. One of the harder parts of mental health undulations is having to speak up about it. For this process I can offer you some snippets of advice that could be the right thing for you.

- **Understand that there is no normal**
  You are not broken, defective or somehow less than a full human being. Mental health is not an on or off switch. It is a constant process. It is not something we aim to fix. It is something we work to help boost and support when it needs it.

- **Try to avoid self-diagnosis online**
  There are plenty of quizzes and questionnaires there, but they are not personalized at all. There is a reason it takes health professionals so long to qualify. There is so much to learn, so why would a five-minute quiz help you? The intersection of surroundings, your personality and your symptoms are too complex for this process.

- **Keep track**
  It may sound bizarre, but I would suggest you keep an eye on yourself. Watch your mood, emotional levels and response to certain situations. This is the best way to see what is causing the way you feel and can provide some answers. Grab a notebook or journal and jot down your feelings and how your mood

has changed. You might not want to discuss it yet, but over a few weeks you will begin to build up a picture of how you feel. This then can be used when you begin to talk about how you feel.

- **Communication is key**
  If you have a strong relationship with a person in your family, then the familiarity of the relationship and familiar setting will help ease the pressure this conversation may create. If you don't have this bond or feel like it could be used against you, then perhaps a friend you trust and know well can work in place of a family member.

  Face to face might feel too intense, and that makes sense. So perhaps a video call could work. The distance might help you to share anxieties, or you could even just send voice notes so you have the space to say everything you need to say without interruptions. There are organizations that you can speak to. For example, if you text 'Shout' on 85258, you can receive free, confidential advice via text and support 24 hours a day, seven days a week.

Helpful Services You Need to Know About

There is only so much one person can go through alone. For many of us we would all like a little more help. Standard advice suggests starting with your GP, but we all know that the NHS can be a very tricky system to enter as a gender diverse person. So, in order to provide you with the help you may need now, or in the future, I have compiled some amazing organizations that are there for you!

- **Anxiety UK, anxiety.org.uk**
  A user-led service for those who are struggling with stress and anxiety, this service is not LGBTQIA+ exclusive, but offers instant advice and help for those who are struggling.

- **CALM, thecalmzone.net**
  CALM (campaign against living miserably) is the leading movement to prevent suicide. It offers a helpline and web chat service seven days a week to help those struggling with suicidal thoughts, and also a service for those affected by suicide.

- **Kooth, www.kooth.com**
  Kooth offers free, anonymous mental health support, targeted at younger audiences. It also acts as a signposting service for other mental health services available across the UK.

- **Samaritans, samaritans.org.uk**
  Samaritans is a charity aimed at helping anyone in emotional distress. It has dedicated helplines and offers help for free whenever you need it.

- **Shout, giveusashout.org**
  Shout is the UK's free mental health text support service, which offers free, impartial advice every day of the year.

- **Stonewall Housing, stonewallhousing.org**
  Since 1983, Stonewall Housing has worked tirelessly to provide safe housing solutions for the LGBTQIA+ community. It provides specialist services for all the intersections of the community in London.

- **Switchboard, switchboard.LGBT**
  Switchboard offers a listening service via calls, email or messaging to help you. It covers all the intersections of mental health and is LGBTQIA+ specific, with all volunteers self-defining as LGBTQIA+.

- **Young Minds, www.youngminds.org.uk**
  Young Minds is the UK's leading mental health charity for young people. It has lots of resources online for young people and parents too.

How to Calm Anxiety

In my role as a content creator, I speak to a lot of people from all backgrounds. One of the common themes when it comes to mental health is anxiety. It is one of the things that plague us as humans and has differing effects on us all. For me it is the sickening (not in a good way) pull of worry that keeps me awake at night and the fear that no one really appreciates me, which can leave me in a state.

Anxiety is so great at its job because it can target memories as well as things happening right now. It can even try to make us see an altered future. There are many symptoms and many reasons we can suffer with some of the effects of anxiety, and perhaps some of the conversations we have had in these pages may have caused some anxiety. With this in mind, I wanted to share some small interventions that can help calm anxiety.

In Chapter 13 we explored the benefits of sleep, drinking enough water and using balance as a good way to maintain a healthy lifestyle. Using this is a great place to start.

Mindfulness is one thing people often quote as being helpful for anxiety, but I have found it patchy at best. It relies on the ability to overcome internal thoughts, and in the depths of stronger anxiety symptoms this is not always possible. Breathing exercises can work, though. They offer a physical road block to deeper symptoms. Try box breathing, which I shared with you earlier (p.189).

Anxiety can manifest itself in panic attacks. Perhaps they are overlooked as many assume they are just fixed by breathing heavily into a paper bag. Actually a panic attack can manifest itself in many forms. To ease its passing, try to focus on your breathing. Distract your senses by eating strong flavours like a mint or chewing gum. Move somewhere quiet and either focus on being calmer or work on distracting yourself by counting or stamping your feet to the rhythm of your breathing.

Of course, if the symptoms of anxiety increase or become more severe, please seek further help. Your GP can help, but if that doesn't feel possible for you, Mind (www.mind.org.uk) has advice and support available to help.

Where to Access Therapy

When engaged with in the right ways, therapy is a useful method of maintaining and boosting mental health. Of late, to some, therapy has become a trend item, to signal one's 'wokeness'. They forgot to mention that therapy can be tough, be confusing and provide more questions than answers. I truly believe that everyone can benefit from talking therapies – essentially, having conversations with someone who is impartial and removed from your life. They can offer advice that will make a real difference. It can be perfectly tailored to your needs.

Therapy can cost a lot of money, but you can receive free

therapy through the NHS. You can be referred by a GP, or you can use the IAPT (Improving Access to Psychological Therapies) to refer yourself in England. You need to be registered with a GP, but once you have done that, you are in control of how you access what you need. They offer support using a wide range of psychological therapies that are all completely free.

Many LGBTQIA+ organizations across the UK can help you access therapy for free. For example, in the northwest, LGBT Foundation (LGBT.foundation) has a service where you can fill out a form to access talking therapy and counselling that only requires you to be registered to a GP, but no other NHS interaction.

If you need this kind of service quicker, then paying may be an option if you can afford it. A great way is online, through services like Talk Space (try.talkspace.com). They offer differing levels of access dependent on what you can afford, and you can tailor it to your specific needs.

Hate Crime Help

Sadly, we are seeing unprecedented levels of hate crimes. This is due to many social and economic reasons. Tragically, the LGBTQIA+ community faces the brunt of these attacks. More and more community members have been subjected to some of the ugliness in the world.

A recent Stonewall report found that two in five trans people have experienced a hate crime or incident because of their gender identity. One in ten LGBTQIA+ people have experienced online homophobic, biphobic and transphobic abuse or behaviour directed at them personally. It is pertinent because I have been subject to hate crimes and know others that have too.

Many and most hate crimes go unreported due to fear and lack of faith in the justice system in the UK currently. This leaves all the power with the perpetrators of the crime. In this instance there is a wonderful organization that you need to know about. You should never be alone when dealing with situations like this. Galop (galop.org.uk) offers support for LGBTQIA+ people who have experienced hate crimes, domestic abuse and sexual abuse. It has specialist trans advocacy services and you can reach out to them via a referral form on its site for free, impartial and confidential advice to help you.

Not Quite the End

As Adele once sang, 'this is the end'. Naturally, that would make this the conclusion. If you have read any of these pages you may have worked out that this is not really the end. Moreover, this is just a junction, or a fork in the road, if you like. The journey continues from this point, and for many of us exploring our identities together in these pages, this is just the beginning really.

If I could offer you any parting advice, it would be this. You are never alone – even though it may feel like it. I hope you see that there is a whole world filled with flourishing gender diverse people. The unique and wonderful nature of our identities, journeys and past experiences create a web of interconnected support systems.

This brings me to my next point – never suffer in silence. The narrative that is woven throughout this book is ownership of self. It also, sadly, has covered the ways in which we have been made to suffer. The very nature of our suffering is unique to us. However, that means that the community around you will understand your suffering. These are the people that are best placed to help. We may have limited time for constant conversations with cishet people about pronouns, yet we will always have time for each other – community will always come first.

The pages of this book should give you hope, showing your place in society as a valid and wonderful person. The next steps after the book are up to you. They may feel shaky at first, but confidence and comfort will follow in time. This process is greatly supported by believing in yourself. In Chapter 12 I explained that life is like a set of stairs. While self-belief will not make life vastly different, it can make it easier. Think of belief in yourself as a really well-built banister for your stairs. That banister will give you support as you climb the stairs of life and will offer you comfort and confidence in your steps.

The addition of that supportive banister of belief should provide you the courage you need to be able to shrug off some of the harder aspects of your existence. I hope the time we have spent together in these pages has provided you with an ability to see your worth. Just as I have played my role in helping gender diverse people, you will also do that as you blossom into the person you truly are.

Growth is inevitable, and I hope this tome has allowed you to do just that. We can be very protective of our sense of self. In doing this, we can limit our growth. Ignoring opportunities to blossom is something we all do. However, I hope that you have seen a route through these moments of self-doubt. I spent a long time at the beginning of this process thinking that I couldn't write a book. I nearly denied you this very book due to fear. That is a very real example of how limiting your own growth can go on to limit benefit for more than just yourself!

I am aware that this book may have missed the mark with you. Perhaps it didn't strike a chord. It may have created even more questions than you had when you picked it up originally. This is all okay. This book cannot be the only resource. As we have explored in detail through these pages, there is no one way to be non-binary.

It would be unfair of me to assume this is the perfect and only book non-binary people need. It would also be unfair of me to place that much pressure on my elegant yet sturdy shoulders. It is clear that the gender diverse community needs a raft of options.

It is very important to me that this is one of the *many* resources you use to aid your self-development. With that in mind, I would like to offer you some further reading. These are resources that can offer a different take, an alternative experience and perhaps a differing viewpoint that you may need.

- *What's the T?* – Juno Dawson
- *Burgerz* – Travis Alabanza
- *Gender Explorers* – Juno Roche
- *Coming Out Stories* – Emma Goswell and Sam Walker
- *Trans Survival Workbook* – Owl and Fox Fisher
- *Queer Body Power* – Essie Dennis
- *Beyond the Gender Binary* – Alok Vaid-Menon
- *Non-Binary Lives* – Jos Twist, Ben Vincent, Meg-John Barker and Kat Gupta
- *They/Them/Their* – Eris Young
- *This Book Will Make You Kinder* – Henry James Garrett
- *Sabotage* – Emma Gannon

I am not the best at goodbyes – I never have been. So I won't say goodbye. Instead I offer you these final words: never be anything less than yourself, you owe it to you.

Until we meet again my darling, I love you lots like jelly tots, big love to you...

Ben Pechey

Acknowledgements

When I started this process, the acknowledgements were the furthest thing from my mind. It took me a long time to believe that this project would reach this stage, but here we are, kids! As this is my first chance to write acknowledgements, I fear they may be a little long. However, it must be said that a book is truly not a solo process. There are so many people involved, and this is the time that I must acknowledge them.

Obviously, I must thank the darling Andrew, my editor and facilitator of this entire process. I never knew I had this in me until you asked me to find it. Thank you for allowing me to grow in ways I never knew were possible. I appreciate all the hard work put in behind the scenes at Jessica Kingsley Publishers.

To all the lovely people who gave their time and experience to be interviewed for this book, I thank you from the bottom of my heart. Your words will make this book a better resource than I could have ever made alone, so thank you for reminding me of the strength that lies in our community.

I want to take the time to thank my divine illustrator Sam. You have brought my words alive in the form of your stunning art.

You have enriched this book so much, and I am so thrilled you were able to lend your expertise to my humble thoughts.

To my beloved mum, Ruth, for always having my back. Your continued support and love is something I hold very dear and gets me through many a dark day. I also love that you helped me through every part of this process, from the proposal, through stressed afternoons and even proofreading the draft manuscript. I'm not sure I could have done this without you, and I know you'll disagree, but for once I really am right, so thank you.

To my long-suffering photographer, Rachel, who also happens to be my favourite (and only) sister. Thank you for helping me grow my passion into the way I am now able to live my life. My blog is where this book was born, and without your support, I would have never got here. Thank you for putting up with my occasional grumpiness, and diva-adjacent demands. I will be forever grateful to you for your dedication and love, so thank you.

Thank you to my grandparents, David and Shirley, who supported me through higher education, allowing me always to be able to give my all, and who helped me get to the places I am today.

Helen, for very sadly reminding me of the shortness of our lives, and giving me the drive to always continue – we never know what is around the corner.

To the tutors and staff I encountered during my degree, especially Lynda Fitzwater, Liz Wilson and Simone Konu Rae – your encouragement is something I'll never forget.

The adage it takes a village is never truer than when it comes to my career, so thank you to the angels at The Tape Agency for allowing me to believe in myself professionally and for being the professional family I have always needed.

To all the brands, businesses and individuals who have worked with me. It has been affirming having the trust and belief of brands I grew up with pass the microphone to me for a short while, so thank you for being on this journey.

To you, the reader, and the community. Thank you for being an inspiration to me and the driving force that I have needed. I am here as a voice of reason and education, but every day you teach me something new and make me a better advocate for our community. So thank you from the bottom of my queer heart.

Oh, and to all the people who tried to pull me down, or told me I was worthless. Look how far I have come...

Puzzle and Question Solutions

Chapter 5 Self-Love Word Search Resolution

```
a m l t d o o t s r i a p e r e q h u l
b s p v i e e o v o i c e t s b e e q d
y o t e f a n n e s p a c e x c s f o r
z l q s r y z j o y b v l b e l i e f p
i a h s m m t v c z b r l z x a e c l y
h c e s f y i i z u d z o z g u v o s f
i e r s y j v s l x i n v w t g r m b z
o b u e s x f f s a o m e p r h e p q d
o f o n f q k i h i u c p r u t s a q b
w z n d r b b x s v o q b o h e e s e p
h g o n k n a u c y p n e t r r d s f h
a d h i g d l r a t d l h d c t j i n k
s n p k d c a e l i r f e e t e a o z n
t e b y n z n s m v i l q a m p p n t e
h k l i t y c c b i h e x t s i e s t w
m e g k r w e w d t d n r p y u t a e i
t n a y u t o x q i g h b y y o r u c r
g i m z s r q n r s x g s k w n w e q e
u h i j t z x p n o i t a i c e r p p a
a s s h l e u c l p w o p g l r t m x s
```

Chapter 6 Self-Awareness Crossword Resolution

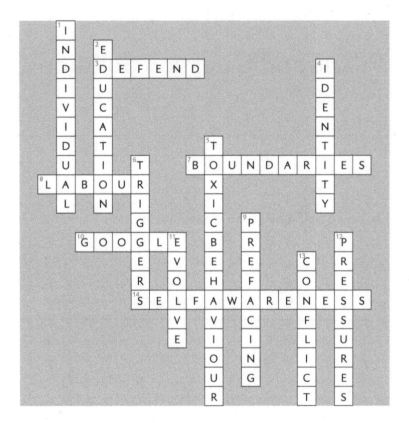

Chapter 11 Social Media Guess Who

Steve
SWIPE LEFT:
Is a massive virtue signaller
Is actually jamming feeds with unnecessary content!

Otto
SWIPE RIGHT:
Calls people in, not out
Doesn't gatekeep
Good egg!

Kit
SWIPE LEFT:
Is gatekeeping
Is making the landscape less diverse in the name of activism

Jane
SWIPE LEFT:
Loves cancel culture
Is too selfish
Bad attitude

For every one good person, there are about three bad! Even I can't manipulate this shit!

Chapter 13 Distraction Word Search Resolution

```
p a n t a m j g n b p o v r k v u o a b
g x q w a t e r l p l a n f t f o n b w
f b m j e d i s t u o z e r u t a n m a
p d s e u a t n e t n o c c i z x d j l
q e u r j n k c n b k z s k d c j b a l
h z e c l m d e o l z v y c i o a y i a
z i n l w a w u r e p e t i t i o n g c
p n o x s m i s l c p s s i d e r m l e
u a i e d i s t r a c t i o n e h u a q
v g t h v v f t z o t k y o j n b k t a
j r c x f m r u g e k i w u v i c d s r
c o e o w o i m t r h y o z u t n d o g
h q p d f j x i a m o e k n s u y x n y
f o s m k g p b e n b m a l s o e b n v
t v o m v s b d m r b h i l u r k v d d
x c r m e a i h e q i u s t t x o o l w
w j t r a t j x c l e z h g s h s p g u
m x n n a w h d b f s a e r a c f l e s
i w i t v z x g n i h t a e r b e b v q
l h e h s z j z e c n a l a b l u m y z
```